PRAISE FOR *THE SONG IN THE SQUALL*

"*The Song in the Squall* is a unique and musically-charged tale of wanderlust, growing pains, and bonds that run deeper than the sea."
—Jessica McHugh, author of *Rabbits in the Garden* and the Darla Decker Series

"Great young adult literature often explores the power of friendship. Add a component of magic, and the quest to find out what is really important in life, and you have the basic elements of a great story. Add a sharp, focused writing style and you have Nathan Singer's *The Song in the Squall*. Original and compelling—do not miss it!"
—Carolyn Haines, *USA Today* bestselling author of the Sarah Booth Delaney and Pluto's Snitch mystery series.

"Nathan Singer's *The Song in the Squall* is a glorious book, redolent with the taste of the salt sea and the sharp odor of an approaching thunderstorm. Dya is a young girl making the difficult transition from the depths of the sea to the land, finding friendship as well as conflict along the way. Dya, Molly, Malik, Mary Louise, and the other characters are drawn with emotion and an unflinching honesty that grips the reader's heart and refuses to release it until the final, bittersweet conclusion. Open this book and follow the shimmering footsteps in the sands. You won't regret the journey!"
—Stephen Leigh, author of *Crow of Connemara* and *A Fading Sun*

The Song in the Squall

BOOKS BY NATHAN SINGER

A Prayer for Dawn
Chasing the Wolf
In the Light of You
Transorbital
The Song in the Squall
Blackchurch Furnace

Nathan Singer

The Song in the Squall

Copyright © 2017 by Nathan Singer
First Down & Out Books Edition November 2020

All rights reserved. No part of the book may be reproduced in any form or by any electronic or mechanical means, including information storage and retrieval systems, without permission in writing from the publisher, except by a reviewer who may quote brief passages in a review.

Down & Out Books
3959 Van Dyke Road, Suite 265
Lutz, FL 33558
DownAndOutBooks.com

The characters and events in this book are fictitious. Any similarity to real persons, living or dead, is coincidental and not intended by the author.

Cover design by Philip Rogers

ISBN: 1-64396-121-7
ISBN-13: 978-1-64396-121-7

*So we'll walk down the shoreline one last time together
The wind blowing our wandering hearts like a feather...*
—David Gray, "Shine"

I had stayed too long in the deep this time.

My lungs ached as I pushed hard, up and up, miles or more, through ever warmer, lighter water. The thinner it got the more I longed to take that first great gulp of new air, my first in many months...or longer. The closer to the surface I climbed, the more I could feel my body changing. The weaker I felt, the harder it was to push upward. The more my lungs throbbed in pain. I had stayed down too long. I tried not to panic.

Just a bit further now...

I noticed my feet for the first time, the first time in a long time. They felt alien to me, awkward and less than helpful in the ocean's current. No longer gliding, I was simply swimming. One step up from flailing.

Almost there...

With one final, desperate push I broke through the surface, blowing out from my mouth a spray of deep sea mist, then gasping and shuddering. I wanted to scream, but I resisted, knowing that it could be dangerous...for me, or anyone who may be within earshot. The most difficult part had passed, but still I had to fight the undertow to swim ashore. And already the deep called me back. The desire to plunge back down again was almost unbearable. I yearned for the heavier, richer water, the endless blackness. But I didn't go. My mind was made up. I'd waited for this for far too long...and I'm never going back again.

Her voice was nothing but snarling, guttural barks at first. Harsh and incomprehensible. But I knew it would get clearer. I knew it would soften. I knew my ears would adjust soon enough, and I would remember. I would remember what the words mean, and how to listen. I would grow to love the sound again. And she knew to keep talking until her words finally came through clearly. And at last they did.

"I knew tonight would be the night," I heard her say. The hour was very late, and I could barely move, resting instead on my knees on the smooth but unforgiving pebbles, my arms squeezing tight against my breasts. Rocking. My equilibrium in a tailspin. The waves crashed behind me against the stone beach, reaching out for me, just barely missing my toes. The wind stabbed hard against my back. She threw a blanket around my wet, naked, shivering frame.

"Somehow I knew," she said. "I knew it would be tonight. Of all nights. Somehow."

She pulled a vine of seaweed from my hair, cast it aside, and then softly touched my head with her fingertips.

"Somehow. Somehow I knew."

I looked up at her finally, and was startled by her face. Lined and creased. I nearly failed to recognize her. She was older. Much older. Old. Had I really been away so long? She must have seen the question in my eyes.

"Fifty-one years," she said. "It's...yes it has. It has been fifty-one years. I know you don't understand that. But for us...well, it's a pretty long time."

I didn't understand how time works on land. I still don't. I have tried my best to comprehend it, and I likely do better than the rest of my people...

I'm so sorry, Mary Louise. I'm so sorry.

But I'm also likely the only one of my people who cares to understand.

Please forgive me. I didn't realize. I didn't know.

She struggled to sit by my side on the pebble beach, her

bones creaking a bit, not what they once were. Finally she made it into a cross-legged position on the ground, and wrapped her arms around me. I fought to regain my breath and balance. I leaned into her and she cradled me in her arms. I wanted desperately to speak to her, but I knew I had to wait.

It's too early yet.

I didn't know what the sound of my voice would do to her. I wasn't sure I could control it yet.

I hope you understand.

We listened to the ocean crashing, lit only by the dim cast of her porch light several yards away.

"I've missed you," she said. "I've missed you every day."

I nodded in reply.

"Come on," she said, "let's get you inside."

At her round oak kitchen table I sat, eating a garden salad with my fingers, as she put a kettle on the stove for tea. It's always hard to re-adjust to land food, but I do enjoy it. I sat wrapped in a large, pink housecoat, and nothing else. Nothing in the house was suitable for my body. It looked ridiculous I'm sure, but it felt soothing. Her cat beneath the table rubbed his cheeks against my bare feet, soft as they were like the skin of a newborn baby.

Mary Louise gave me what she called "the nickel tour" of her life since last we met : College. Her brother's death in the Vietnam War. Marriage. Divorce. Various moves around the country. Her eventual move back to Maine. Friends who have come and gone. And gone for good. The death of her baby boy in utero. The end of marriage number two. All in a very casual voice.

I moved to stand so I could embrace her, but stopped myself.

I don't think she's ready just yet.

I wondered if she knew that telling me about her various moves about the country was unnecessary, as I could always sense where she was. No matter how far away from me she may have been. I could always feel her. And she must have had some sense of me too.

"Somehow I knew you would be coming tonight."

It was time...

"So," she said turning toward me, teakettle in hand, "if my figuring is close to accurate at all, I'm thinking that you're probably around ninety-seven years old. Or somewhere in that neighborhood."

I nodded. I didn't really know what she meant, but it sounded reasonable. And I didn't know why it mattered.

"But..." she said, "you still look like a sixteen-year-old girl. It's really something. And something else. Just like you were...when I was a sixteen-year-old girl too. It's just...so terribly odd for me."

She poured the tea, clucking her tongue at the peculiarity of it all.

"I'm sixty-seven, love," she said. "This is what sixty-seven years old looks like on us."

I smiled. I wanted to tell her that she still looked beautiful to me. As beautiful as the first day we met, when we were both little girls. But "beautiful" is a difficult word. And I had to still be mindful of my pitch, the potential violence of my voice.

I decided it was worth a try.

"Stlllll..." I whispered, making my best attempt. "Stlllll bitifllllllll..."

She smiled for the first time, and in a flash she looked like the same young girl I remembered. But the smile turned sad, and then it was gone, and she was older again.

"So is this it?" She asked. "Is this really the time? After all this time? Are you finally...staying...for good?"

I nodded, and her face lit up again for just a moment...then sank back to a wistful melancholy.

"Better late than never, I suppose."

"Pleasssse...M'ry Leesss," I struggled, in whisper, to say her name. "Pleassse...f'give me..."

"I don't blame you, Dya," she said with a dismissive wave of her hand. "I don't blame you at all. And you know, I actually look older than I really am."

She sat down across from me, offering me a buttered sugar cookie. I took it, but did not yet take a bite.

"I think it's the wind coming off the sea," she said. "It smacks hard, you know. It ages you."

I nodded.

"It's just...I have waited for this for so long...For so, so long...and now...now that you are really here...I just don't know what to say to you. I mean...It's not like I can ask you how you've been. You know?"

I shrugged.

"Oh what the hell. How have you been, Dya?"

I shrugged again.

"I mean to say...there've been times when I thought that maybe I had...imagined you. Do you know what I mean? That you didn't really exist. That you were just a...hallucination. Just a pretend friend for a lonely little girl with an overactive imagination. Part of me didn't want to...part of me is still afraid to see you again. Happy as I am to see you now."

I'm afraid too! I thought. Why do you think it took me so long to come back?

We sat in thick silence for a while, as the question we both dreaded so hung heavy in the air overhead. Finally she asked:

"Do you think, once they realize you're gone, they will come looking for you?"

"P...puh...perhaps," I said, raising my voice slightly above a whisper, exercising my vocal cords a bit.

"Do you think they'll be angry?"

"My people don't...get angry...as...you know...the word," I replied slowly, but with increasing confidence. And a bit more volume.

"But they do get angry in their way."

"Yes."

"And they get violent."

"Yes...I suppose."

"Very violent."

"Yes...but...they don't...want to draw attention...Not worth it."

"Might they come on land and hurt someone?"

"No," I said.

But I didn't really know for sure. My people are...

"Would they punish you?"

...inscrutable...

I shrugged.

...unpredictable in foreign spaces.

"Might not care at all," I said.

"Would they want to...hurt me?"

She looked very old to me when she said that.

"Never let...them hurt you," I said. I reached my hand across the table. She took it. Her hand was so delicate and thin, skin sliding loosely across bone. I lifted the cup with my other hand and drank a sip of tea, savoring the warmth I had not tasted in what I had come to understand was over half a century. We sat, holding hands across the table.

"So," she said finally. "What's your plan?"

"Plan?"

"You're going to need a plan, Dya. Whomever you are underwater, love, you're a teenage girl up here."

"Yes."

"So then...what do you want to do?"

I didn't know. I just wanted to stay.

"Fit. I think. In. Fit in."

"Well, all right," she chuckled. "But, honey, it's not that simple."

"Why?"

"Do you want to go to school?"

"If that's what is done."

"Okay...so who do we say you are then? My granddaughter? Do we just hope that nobody asks too many questions?"

"Why should they care?"

"Because, sweetheart," she laughed, "everyone is mixed up in everyone else's business up here. All the time. That's why.

Trust me, they will ask questions."

"I just want to be here. I want to be on land," I said, clear, and in full voice.

"From now on and forever. Whatever I have to do. I want to stay with you. Please let me stay."

"I want you to stay."

I took a bite of the cookie. It was dry and harsh in my throat.

"More tea?" I asked, struggling not to cough or choke. She stood to fetch the kettle and two fresh tea bags.

"Well," she announced, "we're going to have to get you some clothes, first of all. And I know you're a quick study, so that's good. I can get you up to speed on basic mathematics, and traffic signals, and that sort of thing. Spelling. We did that once, remember?" I nodded. It was long ago...but not really so long to me. "It's like riding a bicycle," she said, and then stopped short and laughed to herself. I didn't understand what was funny, and didn't ask.

"I'm thinking, though," she continued, "that you're not going to be able to go out for a while. You've got a bit of...transforming yet to do."

"Is it so obvious as all of that?" I asked.

"Well, love," she chuckled. "Your silver fingernails? Your silver toes? Folks might just think it's nail polish. The silver hair? Hmmmm, could be 'punk' or something. But your eyes, love. Your eyes..."

"What's wrong with my eyes?"

She smiled. "You haven't seen your reflection in a very long time, have you. Come with me."

She led me to a small mirror hanging in her hallway, and I saw my reflection for the first time in fifty-one years. My cheekbones were sharper than I had remembered. My skin like buttermilk. And my eyes...my eyes...

"They're gorgeous," she said. "Like emeralds. But they're so sharp. They'll be seen as menacing. Alien. They'll frighten people, sweetheart. Try to understand. That's why we had to cover them last time. The sunglasses, remember?"

"All this will fade."
"I know. Just give it time."
"And then I'll look more..."
"Don't say normal."
"Normal."
"They just wouldn't understand," she said. "That's all."
"I remember how it is. I will change. Very soon, I'll blend right in."
"And I'll help you any way I can," she said, laying a comforting hand upon my shoulder. "But as far as teaching you how to be a young person...a teenager...I can't do that. Not anymore."
"Why not?"
"Because, honey, I haven't been a teenage girl in a very long time. And that act is constantly changing routines. Constantly. It is impossible to keep up. Believe me, those people are just as much a mystery to me right now as they are to you. Sorry, love. On that front, you're on your own."

I took a long, hot shower, attempting to scrub over fifty years of salt water from my body. I stared at the array of gels and cream rinses, loofahs and scrubbing stones, unable to make sense of it all. The steaming fresh water felt strange at first, but I grew to love it quickly—as I love so much about this world on land.

Afterward Mary Louise made a bed for me on her couch, and settled herself into an easy chair close by. We turned off all of the lights, and I sang to her in the pitch dark. The sound of the crashing ocean spilled in from the open windows, stirring my desire for the deep once again, which I quickly buried.

It was an ancient song that I sang, one my great aunts taught me. A song meant to lure some sailors away from danger, and others to their doom. I sang, and Mary Louise cried softly from the sound, until she fell fast asleep. The song does that too.

Things Changed in Portland

Back at the cabin, Dya had mostly stayed inside until nightfall. It was exciting, for both of them, keeping her hidden away from prying local eyes like a wild little secret. Just like it had been, so many decades before.

By day they would work on Dya's "lessons," laughing and carrying on. Singing along to David Gray and Ray LaMontagne records. Drinking hot cider and gobbling up great bowls of bananas and cream. Strawberries and chocolate. Peaches and nectarines and Beal's Famous raspberry ice cream.

"There's nothing like this underwater! Nothing even close!"

By the light of the moon they would sit on the beach all night, telling stories and catching up. Mary Louise had lived such a full life on land. Constant change. Joy and sorrow. Highs and lows. Dya could not say the same for herself. In the deep, life was much as it had always been.

It was difficult to be sure, sitting so close to the crashing waves, unable to dive in. Her body ached for it. She could taste the salt on the air. But she fought through it.

And, of course, there were other fears gnawing at her as well.

Are my people looking for me? Can they sense me out here? The more my body changes, the less they will be able to. I'm sure of it. Just wait. Be patient. Be careful.

* * *

Days and weeks passed, summer began its slow fade, and her hair and nails lost their silver (but for one streak behind her ear). Her features softened. Her eyes grew hazel.

"I'd forgotten you're a brunette!" Mary Louise said, quite tickled for the rediscovery.

Finally she could pass. She could fit in. It was time to move.

So they packed up Mary Louise's beaten Honda Civic, gave the cat to a friendly neighbor, and headed off for Portland. For high school and whatever else may await them. Come what may.

It was a thrill, at first, this brand new adventure. Dya looked forward to riding buses, eating in cafés, shaking hands and how-do-you-do.

Hat on my head, shoes on my feet. I want to meet people and to see things and...to be someone new. Someone funny and smart? Someone mysterious and alluring? Who would I be? Who will be there? What more could I learn and do? So much possibility. So much discovery ahead...

The Bayside apartment was small. And cramped.

Compared to what I was accustomed to, any place would be.

The buses were crowded. And smelled from burnt motor oil and stagnant air.

I'll walk whenever possible. I prefer walking anyway.

Everything felt tight. A bit too close.

But that's how it is up here. One can certainly adjust, yes?

Mid-August brought the first day of school.

I don't know what I was expecting...

School was loud and pushy. And cramped. And crowded. And confusing. And smelled from burnt cooking oil and stagnant air.

And mean.
Vicious.
Random.
So this is high school?
In Portland...things were different.

Mary Louise would say, "This, love, is what we call reality setting in."
Reality came and settled right on top of me.

At school, Dya didn't understand what anyone was saying. Not the teachers, not the guards, not the other students. As if they were speaking a completely different language from the one Mary Louise had taught her. And it made no sense at all. There appeared to be some pre-designed structure, some power dynamic in place, but what was it? Did basketball players interact with the debate team? Could cheerleaders be friends with "theater queers"? She could not tell where one clique began or ended, or what made someone "A Crowd" and someone else not. What was it that made gorgeous rich boys like Robert "Robbo" Boucher and Bradford Pitre flash their mile of perfect white smile at one person, and burn someone else with contempt a second later? Dya simply could not add it up in her mind.

What she did understand about her new peers, however, for it was as clear as still water, was that whomever they were and wherever they fell individually upon the spectrum...they did not care a bit for her. Whatever meager value her novelty carried was quickly spent.

Everyone stared at her, and then they ignored her. She would smile, and they would glare. She would try to talk, and they would laugh. She would try to answer, and she would be wrong. So, finally, she decided to just be quiet. And small.

And that just made things worse.

The only person who paid her any attention at all was her Photo lab partner Jimmie Kendall, an "A Crowder" at that, who found her quiet smallness quite a bit of good sport.

He seems to think he can use me as his own personal plaything.

It wasn't merely the cruelty that baffled her. It was the abstracted nature of it all. The gleeful celebration of arbitrary malevolence. Whatever flaws Dya perceived in the culture of her people, and they certainly were many, at least there appeared to be a reason behind most of what they did—archaic though those reasons may have seemed. But acclimating herself to this manufactured chaos was going to take some getting used to.

I thought I was ready…but I sure wasn't. The fear hit her right away—*I'm failing to adapt.*

The ability to adapt, quickly and thoroughly, was the one thing she did well (except for using her voice, which should could not do here at all). It was a great talent her people possessed, this quick adaptation: necessary for survival in the world of the ocean. Without it, they are dead.

Without it, I'm nothing. And I'm failing.

In the deep, Dya's name was good. Her family was held in high regard, her father in particular (*wherever he is*). Dya herself was rare for her particular talents, which would likely make her leaving so much more of an offense and an outrage. An insult. Perhaps even a punishable one.

And with all that, she found herself, quite in spite of herself…homesick.

Fearful. Lost. Staring out across the waiting water. Wondering what will be for her. Wondering what *could* be. Wondering what folks were doing back home.

Nothing! That is what they are doing! The same nothing they've done for a thousand years yet. Hunting the same. Hiding the same. Reciting the same worn tales of ancient glory. Mindless…redundant…endless, black emptiness…

Dya knew that, had she chosen to stay underwater, all of the ocean could have been her playground. *Certainly no shortage of adventure there, I suppose.* And she would always have the peace of the deep awaiting her. *Endless, black nothingness...*And a gorgeous, opiate serenity to call home.

That is not what I want for my life. I have made my choice.

What Was Out There

I was always too curious. I had been warned countless times not to stray too far off on my own.

—Stay with the pod, Dya—they would say. But I never did. I couldn't. I was too restless. I just knew there was something off in the distance. Something wonderful and new.

Most of my people never venture anywhere near land. The majority will never even see a coastline off in the distance. They will surface for air, take in a great breath, and then quickly dive back down. As such, most of my people don't even believe that there are such things as people on land.

—Land people—Ha—The very thought—

With walking legs and everything. Like a crab, but just the two. Nothing but the stuff of myth and legend to be sure. Tales of psychotic, harpoon-wielding boatmen abound in our folklore, some of whom are apparently part bobcat, part bear, or part bird, depending upon who is telling the tale. Not that many of them have ever seen a bear or a bobcat, or any birds at all but seagulls that have flown out to die.

It makes sense, after all. The ocean is vast. Land above the surface is relatively sparse. Most of it would be uninhabitable even if people could live there. They would have to be monstrous creatures to survive in such an environment, so the common thinking goes.

But I always wondered what was out there. What was it

like? How would it be to walk...to run...on feet and legs? To "dance," as I had heard mentioned? I had known of no one to have ever done it, except for my uncle Kalae. He never spoke of it, and I was admonished never to ask. If I were to ever know, I'd likely have to discover it all for myself.

Loving the warmer water at the surface as I do, I had to figure: The further you went in, the warmer it would be. It was inevitable that one day I would head off in search of land. But even my wildest flights of fancy could not have prepared me for I would discover once I did.

The New Girl Here

"So who's the new fish, eh?"

Molly looked up from tying her checkered Chuck Taylors, tucked her oily, violet-streaked hair behind her ears, and squinted down the lunch table. She needed glasses. Her dad couldn't afford them. So she faked it, and forced her eyes to focus. The blur became less fuzzy and Molly saw her, sitting alone, head down, her long brunette hair hanging around her like a death shroud.

"Some chick in my photog class," Molly said to Ethan. "Sixth bell. Diane...I think? Debra? Something like that."

"Looks a bit...lost," Ethan said.

"She missed the first, like, week and a half of school. Don't know a thing about her. Never talks. I think she's foreign. Maybe."

Ethan was Molly's friend. One of exactly three. Ethan, his girlfriend Sarah, Molly, and her long time best friend/now new boyfriend Malik were *those kids*. The ones never noticed at school except to be tripped, pushed, mocked, or threatened. "It's a crucial role we play in the overall school dynamic," Molly would say. "In the grand scheme of things, they couldn't function without us."

"Foreign, eh?" Ethan said.

"Maybe. I don't know."

"Interesting...interesting..."

"Whatever."

"Y'know, Moll," Ethan said, his mouth full of PB&J on white, "dat gurl mi' jush be...hol' on." He swallowed hard and continued: "That girl might just be the godsend we've been waiting for, eh."

"What are you talking about?" Molly replied opening her book bag. Her heart sank as she realized that she'd left her brown-bag lunch on the counter at home. Her dad fixed her lunch for her every morning (presumably to make up for whatever else he may have been lacking in the parent-skills department). It was never a great lunch, but he did the best he could.

"Let me have a pretzel," Molly said. "And where's Sarah, eh?"

"She's sick today," Ethan answered, holding open his bag of pretzels and offering it to Molly. "That's the official story and we're sticking by it. It's got nothing to do with her alcoholic mother crashing her car into a mailbox at two forty-five this morning. Nothing at all." Ethan stopped for a moment and laughed dryly to himself, absently flicking at his lip ring with his tongue. "So anyway," he continued, "this new chick. The way I figure it, the cretins and jock heads are likely bored of screwing with us, eh? They've been waiting for a new chew toy for quite some time. And hey! Right? I mean look at her. Can't even see her face. God only knows what she's plotting. She looks a helluva lot more *Columbine* than we do, eh."

Columbine was the official tag on anyone who looked, dressed, or acted slightly left of the norm. Molly and her friends certainly qualified. And once someone was labeled as such, it was open season. Thanks to the school's "zero tolerance" policies, it was no difficult task to get a fellow student suspended or expelled if there was even a suspicion that said student would be engaging in antisocial behavior on school grounds. So the 'A Crowd' had taken it upon themselves to purge the school of *undesirables*. "Big of them, eh?" Molly would say. "They are true heroes." Molly and her friends were some of the last of the hunted freaks left.

Just that morning Molly had been shoulder-shoved into the

lockers with a, "Heads up, Columbine." She quickly looked around to make sure Malik wasn't around. Molly wasn't the real target, and she knew it. Malik was. She knew, as the A Crowd knew, that if Malik had seen Molly getting hassled he would rush in to "defend her honor," or something like that. And Malik was one fight away from expulsion. Molly was hell bent on making sure that didn't happen, even if that meant getting into a fight herself. She'd gladly throw the first punch if necessary.

She had always been that way. Raised by her father and two older brothers (one now dead, the other serving twenty-five to life), Molly couldn't cop to the girly stuff, even if she'd wanted to. Perhaps that's what made her a target. Perhaps it was because she was poor. Perhaps it was all just random.
Who knows…and what does it matter really…

Molly nibbled on her lunch of borrowed butter-twist pretzels and tried not to glance over at the brunette blur in her peripheral vision. She remembered what it was like to be a new fish. She knew all too well how it felt to be a target. She didn't wish it on anybody; regardless of how Ethan "figured it." Her thoughts were interrupted by a bump to her rump as she was scooted slightly down the bench by a familiar hip.

"What up, homie," Molly and Malik said to one another. She brushed his dreadlocks aside and kissed him on the lips. *God, this still feels so weird.* Molly and Malik had known each other since they were six years old, growing up in adjacent apartments. Their fathers were lobstermen on the same boat for a time. He used to pull her hair and run awkwardly away. She used to throw mud at him. And yet, here they were a decade later smooching under florescent lunchroom lights.

"Take it outside, eh?" Ethan said. "Tryin' to eat here."

Ethan and Malik proceeded to engage in a ridiculously

complicated handshake.

Molly looked back over toward the new girl and said, "I'mma go invite her over."

"What?!" Ethan said, mid-shake. "Are you crazy?"

"What's going on?" Malik asked.

"Moll," said Ethan, "you're gonna blow the whole plan!"

"Sucks to your plan, dude," Molly said. "I'm all about strength in numbers."

"What plan?" Malik asked. "Strength in who-what?"

"Be right back," Molly said, giving Malik a quick peck on the cheek, and proceeded to slide down the bench.

The table was longer than she had assumed, and it occurred to her halfway that she should have just stood up and walked down, instead of sliding all the way on her butt. But she was committed to the slide, and opted to see it through.

Finally she made it, right across the table from the girl. The new girl did not look up at Molly, continuing to hide behind her blanket of auburn hair. She made no indication that she even noticed Molly there, except that she had stopped eating her cucumbers and baby carrots.

"Hi there," Molly said to the new girl. No reply. "*Bonjour. Hola. Salam. Guten tag.*" Still nothing. "*Aloha. Shalom. Namaste.* Sorry, that's all I got. Oh! *Buna ziua.*"

The girl did not respond, but put a cucumber slice in her mouth instead.

"Not Romanian, eh?" Molly asked.

The girl shook her head, chewing softly.

"You're in my photography class, right?" Molly said. The girl nodded. "Pretty cool class, eh? I think so. I mean, I don't really want to be a photographer or anything, but it sure beats Algebra. I'm a guitar player, actually. But it's good to be well-rounded, don't you think?"

The girl continued to chew her cucumber.

"So anyway," Molly continued undeterred, "you see those two sorry lumps up there at the end of the table?"

The girl looked over to her left quickly, noticed Ethan and Malik arm wrestling, and quickly put her head down again. She nodded. "Well, I gotta be honest. The level of repressed homoeroticism masquerading as macho posturing over there is getting a bit much for me to handle. So I thought I'd come down here and talk to you instead."

The girl giggled and looked up at Molly for a quick moment. *She's pretty enough,* Molly thought, noticing her light shadow of freckles over the bridge of her nose, and her soft hazel eyes. *Too pretty to hide it, anyway.* Right behind the girl's left ear was a glittering shock of pure silver hair, a perfect contrast to the dark auburn.

"Wicked highlight," Molly said indicating the silver lock. "How'd you do that, eh?"

The girl covered it with her hand self-consciously.

"Don't know," she said, barely above a whisper. "I don't know why that happened. It didn't used to be like that."

"Why don't you come over and sit with us?" The girl lowered her head again, shoulders squared. "Don't worry," Molly said with a wry smirk, "they don't bite. They're more interested in each other than they are in us."

The girl giggled again, but sat still.

Finally, she nodded.

"Excellent," Molly said. "Come on."

They walked over to Ethan and Malik, who were attempting to listen to music on the same iPod, one ear bud apiece.

"God, dude, this song is wicked killer, eh!" Ethan exclaimed, not noticing Molly or the new girl in the least. Malik did notice, however, and stood up to greet them.

"Guys," Molly said. "This is…is it Diane?"

"Dya," the girl said, barely above a whisper. "Hi."

"Dya, Ethan, Malik."

"Hey there," Ethan said with a quick salute, still rocking out, head banging now with both ear buds. "I hear you're an immigrant, eh."

"I am," Dya replied softly.

"Right on."

"All right, Dya," Malik said smiling brightly and extending his right hand. Dya shook his hand shyly, then awkwardly withdrew. "So where you from?"

"I was wondering that too, eh," Molly said.

Just then the bell rang.

"Nice to meet you," Dya said. "I have to get going."

"See you in photog!" Molly said to the quickly escaping new chick. "Well," she said to her friends with a shrug, "I tried."

Molly and Malik walked down the hall to class hand in hand, Malik with a slight but noticeable limp. They walked on, ignoring the nasty grumbles and murmurs from all around. They weren't sure if it had always been like this, but it certainly felt as if it had. They didn't even notice anymore.

They also did not notice that the new girl was watching them too.

It was Sarah who said, "You know, I think we've earned a four-day weekend." Molly, Ethan, and Malik agreed. So in lieu of class they opted to spend both Monday and Tuesday lounging about on the pebbles of East End Beach at the Eastern Promenade, staring off into Casco Bay and slipping clandestine sips of local ale stolen from Ethan's dad (who had himself stolen it from Shipyard Brewing, where he worked the line).

The foursome had little incentive to bother much with school anymore. Their parents certainly did not seem to care if they went or not. As it was, the ocean was at least as good a teacher, if not better. They'd all likely end up on lobster boats someday anyway.

Only Molly had the guts, or the insanity, to swim.

"Still too cold," Sarah whined, dipping her bare feet quickly into the coastal waters. The boys silently concurred without checking for themselves. Molly called them all out for "wussies," and dove in.

"Who'da thought I'd fall for a girl who's part porpoise," Malik said with a shrug. Indeed, nothing could keep Molly out of the water. Even in the midst of the harshest Maine winter she would at least splash about for a moment or two. The few people in the world who knew (or cared) that she existed were in constant fear for her health. But she was almost never sick.

"Mark my words, you guys," Molly said with no small amount of shiver in her voice, "the ocean heals. I'm telling you. I plan on living forever. And still leave a good-looking corpse!"

"Yuh, okay, Moll," Sarah shouted out to her. "Be sure to visit us in the old-folks home, eh. Where it's *warm*."

It was no small amount of distress for Molly, after her much-needed four-day respite from school, to return on Wednesday and come upon three prominent members of the A Crowd backing that weird new girl Dya into an alcove. Molly considered walking on by and pretending she didn't notice. But seeing the poor girl huddled and terrified against the lockers, trying to hide behind a meager shield of reddish-brown hair, surrounded by two muscled rugby players and one of their bubble-headed girlfriends, Molly knew she had to at least *say* something.

"What's the deal here, eh?" Molly shouted walking over quickly, trying to mask the quiver in her voice with pretend confidence.

"Take a hike, freak," Brad Pitre hissed. "Deal with you some other time."

"Yeah," Robbo interjected, "you really don't wanna concern yourself here."

"It is my concern," Molly said. "Nobody menaces my friend. Now what's going on?"

"Oh, you *would* be friends with this little slut, Columbine," Trina sneered. "This bitch got Jimmie expelled. Lured him into the darkroom during sixth bell on Monday."

Holy crap! Molly thought. *Of all the friggin' days to play hooky!*

Jimmie Kendall was the A Crowd's resident "bad boy," even though both his parents were district court judges. Kendall had been Dya's assigned partner in Photo Lab, but Molly had not noticed any chemistry between them. Not that she had been looking.

"If that cretin got expelled," Molly said, "then I'm sure he deserved it."

The three A Crowders turned toward Molly with white-hot death burning in their six baby-blues. Dya looked up, peeking through her hair, trying to stifle the shaking in her hands.

"Walk now," Robbo growled.

"Okay," Molly said, taking a small step back, sweat breaking across her brow. "You're right, eh. I'm out of order. I'll just leave you to your business."

And without warning, Molly swung all fifteen pounds of her stuffed, army-surplus book bag down onto Trina's perfectly coiffed blonde head. The popular girl screamed and crumpled to the floor in a whimpering heap. Dya quickly darted away down the hall. Robbo and Brad, momentarily stunned, moved to advance on Molly. Molly cocked her leg back, her left boot level with Trina's sobbing face.

"You put one foot toward me," Molly said through clenched teeth, "and my steel toes are gonna go smashing right through her pearly whites." Trina screamed again and covered her face with her hands. "How hot will she look for homecoming then, eh Brad?"

Brad and Robbo took two steps back, their hands up in surrender.

"This isn't over, Columbine."

"Oh, I figured that, eh."

***

Molly sat across from the vice principal at his desk, and knew that she was doomed. He eyed her coldly for what seemed like an eternity before finally breaking the silence.

"Miss Jones," he said in a bland, official voice.

"Yes, Mr. Merriwether?"

"Would you like to tell me what happened?"

"Trina Beckett and her friends were threatening a friend of mine over by the old labs."

"I see. And which friend would this be?"

"Um, I don't...I don't really know her that well."

"Ah. A friend you don't know. That's rather sad, Miss Jones."

"Yes sir. I suppose it is."

"You are familiar with this school's policy regarding fighting, are you not?"

"Yes sir."

"This behavior is very unbecoming of a young lady, you know. Very unbecoming."

"I know."

"You used to be an exemplary student, Miss Jones. Until about a year and a half ago. What on earth happened?"

My life went to hell, that's what on earth happened!

"I don't know, sir."

"Are other students giving you difficulties?"

Difficulties? DIFFICULTIES?!?!

"No, sir."

"Any problems at home?"

Uhhhh...well, lessee. My mom is dead. My oldest brother is dead. My other brother is in prison, maybe forever. My dad is working twelve-hour days straight into an early grave. What do you think?!?!

"No, sir. No troubles at home."

"I ought to expel you, Molly."

"I know."

"Do you want that?"
Kinda.
"No, Mr. Merriwether. Not at all."
"And what in god's name have you done to your hair?"
"Don't you like it, sir?"
"I'm issuing you five demerits and four days' suspension, with a Saturday school on top."
"Thank you, sir."
"If you so much as raise your voice on school grounds again, Miss Jones, you will be out on your rear end. Am I making myself perfectly clear?"
"Yes, sir. Thank you."
"And there is one other thing before you go."
Aw damn...
"Yes sir?"
"Can you explain your absence Monday and Tuesday?"
"Um, I wasn't feeling well."
"I see. Do you have a note?"
"Not with me, no. I can have one tomorrow, though. You can call my father if you like."
"It seems a mister Jefferson, a mister Myers, and a miss Gans were also under the weather these past two days."
"Coincidence?"
"Detention today, and two additional demerits. You are on *very* thin ice, Miss Jones. And lest you think detention today will be a hot disco party, your friends will be serving out their respective detentions on separate days. I highly suggest you shape up. Immediately."
"I will, sir. Thank you."
"Get out of my office. I'm through with you."

The school was abuzz with rumors about the incident of "Jimmie and the new fish." The stories ranged from them simply being in the darkroom for too long, to wild flights of nearly pornographic fancy. Most of the more reasonable versions did involve Jimmie Kendall getting caught in the darkroom with his pants down "pressed against some new chick." Molly's friends were thoroughly unconcerned whatever the case, although Ethan did remark that if the rumors were true he hoped that Dya at least had "used her teeth on that sack of douche."

Dya did not come to sixth bell, but she did show up for detention. As she walked past Molly, she smiled and mouthed "thank you." Molly smiled back, determined to get the true skinny as soon as this waste of time was over with.

After two hours and fifty-seven minutes of continuous sitting and silently staring forward, Mr. Merriwether dismissed the assembled detainees with three minutes to spare.

"I'm feeling generous today," he said. "Don't assume it's a trend, people."

"That guy's a prince, eh," Molly said to Dya as they walked out. "A prince I tells ya."

The two walked awkwardly across the muddy soccer field toward the metro stops. Although she certainly had questions, Molly suddenly felt weird about asking them. So they simply trudged along in silence, trying not to get stuck in the soggy mess.

Finally, Dya said softly, "I really want to say again how much I appreciate you sticking up for me."

"Think nothing of it," Molly said. "We've all done our share of making out with creeps." Although in Molly's case this wasn't really true. The only boy she had ever kissed was Malik. "Certainly no one should be beaten up for it, eh."

"I don't really know what you mean," Dya said, giggling nervously.

"Hey, whatever's good with me, girlie," Molly said with a shrug. "Don't make me no nevermind." Pause. "So...um...is this place different from you last school?"

"Yes."

"Better or worse?"

"Just different."

"Gotcha."

They continued on without a word, their shoes growing heavier with cold water and mud.

"Hey there, Dya," said a voice behind them, cracking the silence. Startled, they turned to see Jimmie Kendall walking out from around the old equipment shed. "No hard feelings, eh?"

"What's the matter with you, Jimmie?" Molly asked with a slight gasp. "You look like nine miles of bad road."

And indeed he did. His straight black hair was damp with sweat, and he looked like he hadn't slept. Two full days of explaining your trespass to two angry judges could likely do that to a person.

"You're one to talk, Columbine," Jimmie laughed bitterly. "Why don't you crawl back to your sewer. There's still some hope for *this* one, eh." He nodded his head toward Dya and walked toward them. Molly looked around the fields. No one in sight. No use in yelling for help.

"I d-don't want...anything to do with you, Jimmie," Dya said, stuttering. "Why don't you just leave us alone?"

"*Us?*" Jimmie replied, scoffing broadly. "Come on, Dya, don't tell me you're hanging with this *thing* here. I mean, yeah, you're a new fish, but you're a decent-looking chick, eh. You could run with a much higher class of people if you played your cards right."

"I don't like being cut, Jimmie," Dya said.

Molly's heart jumped in her chest.

"What's that?" she said.

Jimmie's face went white with red blotches.

"Shut up," he said, scowling.

"Cut?" Molly asked. "What do you mean cut?"

"Jimmie likes to cut himself," Dya said. "Both of his thighs are slit open under two layers of gauze bandaging."

"You weren't supposed to say anything," Jimmie snarled. "You were told not to tell."

"Gosh, Jimmie," Molly said, forcing a chuckle. "I never took you for a cutter, eh. How *goth* of you."

"He's not expelled," Dya continued. "His parents are sending him away. Therapists are going to help him with his problem."

"No problems here," Jimmie said with a crooked grin.

"That's why his pants were down in the darkroom," Dya continued further. "He wanted me to cut his leg. And he wanted to cut me too."

"I *did* cut you, new fish," Jimmie hissed, his eyes suddenly aglow with excitement. "Show her."

Dya slipped off her jacket and pulled up her right shirtsleeve. She removed the white gauze taped to her. There across her forearm was the faintest scratch.

"Impressive," Molly said deadpan.

"What?!" Jimmie exclaimed in disbelief. "I went deep on you! I thought you'd need stitches! How did you heal so fast?!"

"Go home, Jimmie," Molly said. "And get help. You need it."

"I can't go home," Jimmie said. "Not for a long, long time. Thanks to her."

He pulled a butterfly knife from his pocket and flipped it open. The girls stepped back with a gasp.

"Don't worry," he said with a Cheshire grin, "I won't hurt you. It doesn't hurt, does it Dya? It feels wicked *awesome*. A little pinch, and then a rush of endorphins. What do you say, Molly? You're a freaky girl, eh. You into blood at all?"

"Molly, cover your ears," Dya said.

"What?" Molly replied.

"Cover your ears."

"What fo—"

But before Molly could finish her question Dya had thrown

her arms over Molly's head, holding her tight to her chest, and let loose with the most piercing, ear-splitting, bone-rattling, blood churning shriek ever heard on land. Jimmie flew backward onto the muddy grass, flat on his back. He curled up like a pill bug and covered his head, desperately attempting to shield his tender eardrums from the sonic onslaught. He writhed in pain as the noise continued to pummel him.

Once Dya's lungs were empty of air, she removed her hands from Molly's ears. Dogs for a mile in every direction howled, barked and whined.

"Hot *damn*!" Molly said, stunned and panting. "What was *that*, eh?"

"Just something I can do," Dya said, breathing hard through clenched teeth.

Jimmie lay on the ground, clutching his head. Molly bent over, picked up his butterfly knife from the damp grass, flipped it shut, and pocketed it.

"What a day," Molly said. "Score two for the weirdoes!" Jimmie groaned in agony. "Is he gonna...be okay?"

"Eventually," Dya replied, catching her breath.

The two proceeded to walk toward the metro stops once again.

"You should come to my place," Molly said. "I've got some music you gotta hear. You ever sing any metal?"

Molly's place was rather small. Even more so than the apartment Dya and Mary Louise shared. Clean, for the most part, but spare. Just the needed things. And nothing else. Nothing decorative or superfluous. As if those who called it home did not really consider it a home. Molly offered Dya a soda, but she declined. She offered Dya one of her father's beers, but no thank you. Just fresh water with ice. Dya assumed that Molly's father was not around, but no mention was made either way.

"I don't know how much you know about guitars," Molly

said, strapping the instrument on over her shoulder, "but this is a Les Paul. It's wicked heavy to hold, but the tone just cannot be topped."

"It's cool," Dya said with all sincerity.

"My cousin gave it to me about two and a half years ago," Molly said, plucking the strings and twisting the tuning pegs. "Right before he died. I'll never play anything else but this machine here ever again. At least as far as electrics are concerned." She turned up the volume on a little black Crate amp propped up on a wooden school chair. It crackled and popped. Her fingers danced across the strings, as her picking hand stroked downward with startling force. The sound was jagged and abrasive thumping out of the speaker. At once both intricate and primal.

"You're really good, Molly," Dya said. "I'm very impressed."

"Thanks," Molly said casually, though her cheeks turned a rosy hue. "This is pretty much all I do, as pathetic as that is."

"It's not pathetic to pursue what you love. That's never pathetic. I stand by that."

"Preach it, girl," Molly chuckled.

"Ummm...all right." Pause. "Do you...um, do you like Elmore James, Molly?"

"LOVE Elmore James, dude," Molly said and played a short, bluesy scale with vibrato. "I've been wanting to get into some slide stuff, but haven't gotten to it yet. Wicked business." Molly looked up from her guitar. "Color *me* impressed, Dya. How many girls our age you think even know who Elmore James was?"

"Maybe just us, right?" Dya replied, her cheeks blushing as well...from pride, but also a droplet or two of guilt. She could not help but feel just a bit deceptive.

"He was giving up on music anyway, my cousin," Molly said, switching off the amp and setting the guitar down on her bed. "He said he'd had his shot and he had no regrets that it never took off. Good for him, eh? It's good to make your peace, you know. But then, *bang*. Two weeks later, he's dead. Ex-girlfriend plugged him in the back of his head with a .38."

"I'm sorry," Dya said, not knowing what else to say. But for a great-great-great-grandfather when she was very young, Dya had never known anyone to die. At least, none she could remember. And murder simply did not happen in the deep (if for no other reason than the sheer difficulty involved). "That must feel awful. For you I mean. And for him too…at the time. I guess."

Dya hated how awkward she felt. How clumsy her conversational skills were. She simply wasn't used to talking with anyone except Mary Louise.

"What can ya do," Molly replied with a shrug of her shoulders. "Is it tragically poignant? Or just stupid and tragic. I dunno. Who am I to say. People in my family sure do die easy, though. That I know for sure. Mom died in a car crash when I was little. My eldest brother…got into some bad stuff a few years ago and…god, what a mess. We might look like hearty folk, but we're wicked fragile, apparently."

"Well…" Dya said, "not too many people can survive being shot in the head."

"Yuh, that's true all right."

Dya took a sip of water. It tasted like chemical sanitizer and plastic to her, but drank it all the same for fear of seeming rude. Molly touched Dya's single silver lock hanging behind her left ear. Much to her own surprise, Dya did not shrink away.

"Hey, can I braid this?"

"Sure. If you like."

"Wicked."

As Molly proceeded to braid away, Dya looked around Molly's cramped, cluttered bedroom. But for the bed and the posters plastered across every inch of wall, one might be forgiven for thinking it more a storage room than a place someone would want to spend much time. Stacked in each corner were brown cardboard boxes. Most were unmarked, but on more than a few words were scribbled in black marker: *books, gramma's house, photos.* Also: *Davey Jr., Sir Charles,* and *Mom.* Dya wanted to ask what the boxes were for. Then it occurred to her that she probably didn't need to.

"You know Malik?" Molly said as she separated the silver hair into three equal ropes and wove them through one another back and forth. "The guy I introduced you to the other day?"

"Your boyfriend?"

"Yuh…"

"He seems really cool. Cute too."

"He used to live across the hall. When we were kids. But they moved away a couple of years ago. Way before we were ever *a thing.*"

"That's too bad," Dya said with a sly grin. "Think of the possibilities."

They both giggled. Molly did not appear the giggling type, and seemed to take herself by surprise.

"When's your birthday, eh?"

"Uh, February," Dya replied, thinking up a quick lie.

"That's amethyst."

Molly walked across the room to the far corner. There she rustled about in a cardboard box wedged inside the opening of an old, worn roll-top desk. The box was full of CDs. Inside that box was another containing small crystals of myriad colors and shapes.

"Sorry about before, talking about death the first time we hang out and all," she said, carefully considering the selection. "I'm not always so emo. I promise."

"It's okay."

She pulled out a small, purplish rock and grabbed a handful of compact discs from the other. She dropped the discs in the plate of her stereo and the player swallowed them up. She pressed *random* and walked back over to Dya.

"I hope you like this stuff," she said as the music began. "I'm in a weird place with music right now. It's either gotta be so punishingly heavy and so loud that it physically hurts to listen to, or so sweet and whispery that you can barely hear it. Nothing in between."

Her selections reflected just that. Song by song, the sound swung between soft harmonies and acoustic arpeggios, to pounding, screaming and thrashing. And Dya loved every bit of it. And in an odd way, it all reminded her of the music of her people. The music of the deep.

Especially the really low tones...and the really high ones.

Visibly pleased with her new friend's enthusiasm for her favorite music, Molly said, "You can borrow whatever you like, eh. My burner's broken, but anything you wanna take with you, just go ahead."

"Thank you!"

"I'm glad to spread it around."

Dya considered for a moment singing a song for her that she knew...but then quickly thought better of it. Her songs, after all, the songs of her people, were powerful and precious to them. And intimate. Sacred, in their way. Dya liked this girl, and wanted her to be her friend. But she wasn't quite ready to share something like that with her. Not just yet.

Molly proceeded to tie the amethyst stone into the tip of Dya's silver braid.

"There you go, eh. Your birthstone."

"Thank you so much."

"So what's your thing, Dya?"

"My...thing?"

"What brought you to our little corner of the world?"

"The ocean did."

"Of course," Molly said with a nod. "My pop's a lobsterman."

Dya had to quickly figure out what Molly meant by this. *Lobsterman...her father is a* lobsterman...*Oh! Of course. He catches* lobsters.

"That can be a rough way to make a living," Dya said. "Or so I've heard."

"Yuh. It's good work if you're on a decent vessel and it's a good harvest. David's not exactly known for his luck, though. None of us are."

"David?"

"My pops. Since Mom died he prefers that I just call him by his first name."

"My grandmother and I do the same thing."

It's so strange to refer to her that way...

"Your dad works the sea too?"

"Well...yeah. Sort of."

"More of a fisherman?"

For a moment she thought she had heard it as "fish man," and had to struggle against taking extreme offense. Then she realized what Molly meant.

"*Fisherman*," she repeated, with a light chuckle. "Yes..."

"Is he commercial?"

"I'm sorry?"

"A fisherman by trade? Or is he one of those self-sustaining types?"

"You could say that. He's not with us, though. I haven't seen my father in quite a long while. I'm hoping he doesn't come looking for me, to be completely honest."

"Ah," Molly said knowingly, "that kinda scene, eh. What a drag."

"Yes."

"So what's the rest of your family like?"

"They're fine," Dya said, not really wanting to discuss it. "They're really...old-fashioned, you know. Stuck in the old ways." She and Mary Louise had worked out a whole routine and backstory to explain away who she was and where she had come from. But Dya really didn't want to have to say it. She didn't want to have to lie unless it was utterly necessary. "I mean...I suppose they're fine. I don't see them anymore. I just live with...my grandmother."

"You run away?"

"Yes. I did."

"Somebody hurt you?"

"No, nobody hurt me."

"How come you ran off then?"

Dya was silent, not sure of how to answer.

"You don't have to say if you don't want to, eh," Molly said. *Déjà vu...when did I hear that last...*

"I'd really rather not," Dya replied. "I'm sorry."

"Hey, I hear ya, dude," Molly said. "No worries. Sorry to pry. I'm just a really curious person."

"I can relate," Dya said. "Believe me."

They bobbed their heads and tapped their feet to the music as it played. It was the loud stuff this time. It made Dya's blood pump fast.

"You think you could sing like this?" Molly asked, banging her head to the driving beat. "I mean, hell, you sure laid Jimmie out with those pipes of yours! How *did* you do that?!"

"It's a gift," Dya said, rocking out in kind. "And a talent. My aunts taught me."

"I'd like to meet those aunts, eh!"

"No...you really wouldn't."

"I wonder how you'd sound with drums, bass, and guitars behind you," Molly said with a devious twinkle in her eye. "You up for trying it out?"

"Of course," Dya said.

A big, silly grin spread across Molly's face.

"My crew is gonna love you, girlie. I think you just might be the piece our puzzle has been missing."

"It would be my honor," Dya said, sitting up very straight and proper. Molly laughed hard, and after of moment's confusion, Dya did as well.

"You're a pretty strange chick, Dya," Molly said. "And understand, that's a big compliment coming from me."

"Well then thank you, Molly. You're a pretty strange chick yourself."

Upon the Shore

I remember the first day I saw her.

I had swum for many miles on my own. Hours turned to days. I was thrilled to see something, anything, on the horizon at last. The closer I got to the shore, the dizzier I felt, the thinner the water became. I found myself getting greedy with the air, inhaling and exhaling at my leisure, not bothering to hold a full breath. What was the use so close to the surface? When the sun grew hot and hard overhead I stayed below, surfacing again at twilight to swim beneath the stars.

The longest breath I held was to dive down away from the boats, the first boats I had ever seen! And every bit as terrifying as I had been lead to believe. With great speed I swam past them, so close to land now that I could genuinely feel it drawing me ever closer.

Coming up upon the coast at sunrise, the anticipation swelled in me so I thought I was likely to burst, so sure was I that I would arrive upon the shore and find it teeming with people, dancing, running about, digging their toes into the sand. Thank goodness I was mistaken. Who could only imagine what would have happened when they saw me.

Fortunately, it was only she.

Beneath the surface I saw the slope of the ocean floor ascending steadily forward. Slowly I crept in, careful to stay deep enough

THE SONG IN THE SQUALL

to still be able to swim without scraping against the sharp rocks. My nerves jangling and my heart pounding, I eased up to break the surface of the water...

...And there she was. All alone. Seven years old or so (just a few years younger than I would have appeared to her then), in a striped blue and white swimsuit, sitting on a flat stone, dipping her feet casually in the water. I startled and quickly wanted to retreat. But she didn't. She simply smiled and waved to me, as if it were the most natural thing in the world to see a strange girl suddenly pop her head out of the ocean from nowhere. I waved back, and she spoke. It was a guttural, barking sound, but I could see by her kind face that she was simply trying to speak with me. I couldn't understand it, but I decided to say Hello all the same. At the sound of my voice, her eyes grew wide, and then she winced, covering her ears. Embarrassed, I shut my mouth, and sunk low into the water. She laughed and waved me in closer.

As I did so she furrowed her brow, squinting, trying to see my body through the ripples in the water. Catching first real sight of me, she squealed! Terrified, I dove under, ready to shoot back out to sea...when suddenly there was a splash, and there she was underwater with me! Turning to face her, I saw that her eyes were shut tight, little clear bubbles of air escaping her nostrils, her hands reached out in front of her. I took her hands in mine, and we surfaced again.

Off in the distance, we heard a hacking, guttural voice, which was apparently the sound of her mother calling. She pointed over at a crevice in the large stone, and I quickly hid. As she crawled out of the water I heard the sound of hysterical screeching that was, once again, her mother. She turned to me and shrugged sheepishly, waved goodbye and ran off. The bounce of her feet against the ground as she darted away astonished me. It was so seamless, so effortless, so natural. I wanted to do that. I needed to do it. But how?

My mind and heart racing, I tore off back to the deep, and to the one person with whom I needed to speak, the only one I knew to ever walk on land.

I knew he would rebuff my questions, brush me off, tell me to quit being a foolish girl. But I would not be denied. I would wear him down. I would convince him that I would only do it once for curiosity's sake, then never again. I would make promises I had no intention of keeping. For I had had my first taste of land, and my appetite would not be easily satiated. I would explore every bit of it. Perhaps more than any of my people had ever dared before.

My uncle Kalae would teach me how to come to land, whether he wished to or not.

A Little More Time

For Mary Louise, things in Portland were different as well. In Portland, Dya was no longer her special secret. No longer her faraway friend. No longer a joyful memory turned dream come true.

In Portland, Dya was her "granddaughter." Her responsibility. Her charge. Every single day.

"Did you do your homework?"

"I don't understand it. Can you help me?"

"Yes," she'd sigh. "I can try to." But most of it was brand new to Mary Louise as well. Or long forgotten. And after all, what's the point of relearning so much that is obviously of no use? But it had to get done.

So long to the evening talks under the moonlight and stars. I've got Geometry to work on. But perhaps that's just as well. I need to be distracted away from the call of the sea.

They still had fun together. They would shop, or see a show. They would go out to catch a late supper, or grab coffee and tea and peruse old bookstores. But Mary Louise would often get tired.

"You're wearing me out, hon," she said, stopping to catch her breath. "You need friends your own age."

"I'm older than you are!" Dya replied. And they would laugh. But secretly it made Dya sad, and a little angry, when Mary Louise would say things like that. "And anyway, people 'my age' don't like me."

"Well that's their loss, sweetheart. That's their loss."

They sure don't seem to be suffering from a lack of my company.

"It's been a while," Mary Louise said as they cleaned up the dinner dishes. "Do you want to maybe walk down to the water tonight? Just for, you know, a little bit of a change of pace or something."

"I can't," Dya replied. "I have a History test I really need to study for."

"That's ironic."

"I know." Pause. "And besides..."

"The temptation?"

"It's still just too strong."

"Very well," Mary Louise sighed. "I certainly don't want to tempt you."

"I'm sorry."

"That's all right."

"You're disappointed."

"It's fine, hon. You have to do what you have to do."

But it wasn't fine.

"Mary Louise..."

"Yes?"

"Nothing."

"What is it?"

"Forget it."

"Come on now. Don't do that."

"Do...I mean...do you..."

"Do I what, Dya?"

"Do you..."

Do you...resent me?

May Louise had never signed off on being a parent, after all. She had tried that already, many years ago, and she bore the grief and pain of that loss. It caused her to drive her second husband away. No matter how much he pleaded with her not to. No matter how many times he told her that he loved her, and always would. All she felt was that loss, and the sight of him simply kept the wound too raw. So he had to go. She decided that she would rather be alone.

"Do I *what*, love?"

"Do you...want to maybe head to Old Port?"

"You and your sweet tooth," Mary Louise said with a wry grin. "Just like a tourist. I swear, we are keeping Beals in business all on our own."

Laughter.

"I like to do my part for the local economy."

"That's quite a sacrifice."

"Just a little more time," Dya said in earnest. "Just a bit more. Perhaps the need will leave my system for good."

Perhaps it will...Perhaps...

"The pull of the sea really is that strong, isn't it," Mary Louise said. It was not a question.

"I think it already is fading," Dya said.

This was a lie, of course. Or perhaps denial. She longed for the ocean now more than ever. In fact, it was getting progressively worse. And the worse things got at school, the harder it was not to run off head first into the crashing waves. Some nights the intensity nearly drove her mad.

Over the deep end, as it were.

"Do you think you are finally off your people's...what would you call it...radar? Sonar? Have they lost track of you yet?"

"I don't know," Dya replied, trying not to bristle at the word 'sonar.' She hated words like that, as if she were some sort of aquatic beast. "I think so. I think they've pretty much lost their sense of me. But I'm not sure. I've mostly lost the sense of *them*, anyway. At least individually. They're just a dull, collective pulse to me now. Fading little by little, day by day."

An uninvited visit from Dya's people was a fear that they both shared, and with good cause. Every slightly abnormal slap of a wave against the rocks, or growling, gurgling noise in the night could be one or more of Dya's relatives come to call. *And what then?* She shuddered to think. It would always turn out to be nothing, of course. But the fear was ever present.

"I just want you to be happy here, love," Mary Louise said, firing up the teakettle and pouring herself another glass of red wine.

"I *am* happy here."

"That's all I want. I don't want you to regret coming."

"I don't regret anything," Dya said. "I want to be here. I want to be *completely* here."

"You want to be completely..." and she stopped herself, and took a long sip of wine.

"What?"

"Nothing, hon."

Dya suspected that she nearly said "human."

But she didn't. Because she knew better.

But old misconceptions die hard, noisy deaths.

Beautiful and Dangerous

"I wondered if I'd ever see you again," she said as we shared a large bowl of raspberry sherbet amidst the haze of early morning. "But guess what. I was pretty sure I would."
"Did you think that maybe you had imagined me?"
"Y'know, that thought never even crossed my mind!"
Careful to make sure I was fully transformed before I left the water—as I was told to always do—I would stumble out onto land (never terribly sure-footed at the onset), and there she would be waiting for me with clothes to wear.
"It's getting boring up here without you."
"It's boring down there without you."

We spent almost every day together that summer. And every new day she would teach me something I hadn't heard before: a word, a song, a story, a joke. Things she learned at school, and wherever else one might learn. It took a little while, but I adapted to, and finally adopted, her language. It wasn't terribly difficult. Once I was able, I would tell her all about my life underwater, such as it was.
"What do you talk about down there?"
"There isn't really a lot of talking. When you can only speak while exhaling, and conserving your breath is vital, conversations are kept brief and sparse."

"Makes sense... What are the others like?"

"Dull. And solemn. But they're okay, I suppose."

"Do you hate not having anybody to talk to?"

"There isn't much to talk about anyway. I mostly just swim and explore. There is so much. I'll never see it all."

"I wish I could see it too."

"I would take you if I could. It is beautiful. But it is deadly."

"That's what makes it neat. You ever see a shark?"

"Ha ha ha! Mary Louise! I see sharks all the time!"

"What do you do when you see one?"

"I get as far away from it as I can as fast as I can! Wouldn't you?"

"Okay.... Hmmmm... What is the food like?"

"Salty."

We would swim in the ocean, splashing and laughing. We would dance about on the beach, making crazy footprints in the sand. We would sing the songs she taught me. And we would laugh and laugh and laugh at the silliest things.

If someone were to come along I would dash away and hide. And she would come tell me when the coast was clear. And we would fall apart in a fit of giggles.

Mary Louise—my special, secret friend.

Through a startling bit of serendipity, in the time between first seeing her on the rocks that day and my next return to land, three whole years had passed without my knowledge. I simply had no sense of it. It turned out to be all for the better, for as she was seven years old at that first fateful meeting, I appeared to her to be ten or so. And still I did three solid years later.

"But how old are you really?" she asked. "Did you ever find out?"

"I asked my aunt Traydla and she said, 'You've not even yet reached your fortieth year!' As if that were too young to even be

THE SONG IN THE SQUALL

asking such a question."

"Wow!" Mary Louise squealed. "That is so cool, Dya!"

"It is?"

"For sure! I mean...you are older than my parents! But you're still a girl! That's just...I mean...wow! You know? Wow!"

"Yes, I see. Well said."

We laughed and laughed.

At first I was careful never to stay gone from the deep for very long, lest my promise to Kalae was found to be broken. But it seemed that, but for my cousin Treaylin, my absence was barely noticed by anyone. And, for the most part, he was good about minding his own business.

Gradually I began to stay away for longer and longer periods. And still not a word was said to me about it. Occasionally I would hear a rumor that my parents or some of my siblings would be returning. But they never did. And I truly did not much care. I didn't really miss them. I never missed anyone while I was in the deep.

Except for Mary Louise.

Not only did I miss her, I began to sense her. Even in the great hollows of the deep I knew where she was on land. I felt her pulse. She could have moved a thousand miles away and I would have known. I could sense her as easily as I could sense everyone in my pod. To a degree, sometimes I could almost feel her mood. Somehow, in a very short amount of time, we connected.

I found myself spending more and more time on land, and wanting less and less to return to home. I loved the pace of life on land. I loved it all. The sights and sounds and tastes. Oh...the tastes most especially. Fruits and breads and cheeses. It took some time to get used to the new flavors and textures. But once I did, I was hooked forever.

As I said before, it must be in my nature to want to go where I'm forbidden. I am restless. Stasis is stagnation, and stagnation is death (or it might just as well be). And the notion that "Things are the way they are because they have always been such"? That I simply cannot abide. You understand that, don't you?

Secret Tones

Knock knock knock.

"Yuh?"

"Hi, Molly," Dya said through the apartment door. "I brought you your homework."

"Hey thanks, dude!" Molly replied. "Come on in!"

Regardless of how diligently she worked to keep up with things, the four-day suspension was going to set Molly back. Still, it would be worth the effort to at least try and keep pace. Dya had taken it upon herself to go around to all of Molly's classes each day and collect her work for her. It was the least she could do, after all. Plus, it gave them a chance to hang out every day after school.

Dya walked in to find Molly sitting in her near-empty living room, cross-legged on a beaten sofa, playing her Les Paul unplugged.

"You hungry, eh?" Molly asked. "Thirsty? Help yourself. There ain't much in there, but whatever we have, *mi casa es su casa*."

"I'm fine, but thank you," Dya replied. She dropped her book bag by the door, set the stack of homework folders in a creaky, wooden rocking chair with a splintered armrest, and plopped down on the sofa with Molly, exhaling deeply.

"Rough day at the office?" Molly asked.

"It was okay," Dya lied. It was never okay. It would likely

never be okay.

"Jerkfaces laying down the jerkface routine, eh?"

"It's what they do, right?"

"I feel ya, girlie. Been there. But, whatever."

"They just...*really* don't like me."

"Hey, nobody likes me either," Molly said with a shrug. "Cuz I'm *too real*."

They laughed.

"I think they don't like me because I'm not real enough," Dya said.

"See? There's just no pleasing folks."

"Some of your teachers said to email them if you had any questions, and be sure to get the notes you missed from a classmate."

"Not likely," Molly said with a cold chuckle. "And I'd have to head down to the public library to email them. We're not wired up around here. So, nuts to that."

"We don't have the internet at our apartment either."

"It's like we're in the dark ages or something, eh."

"I guess so."

"You see any of my crew?"

"I saw Ethan across the hall, but it was too crowded and he was running late for something, so I didn't talk to him. But he gave me one of these."

Dya held up her left hand with her index and pinky fingers extended into the "devil horns" salute. Molly laughed.

"That means he likes you. You can hang with those guys in my absence. No problem. They're wicked cool." Pause. "Hmmmmm...I guess *cool* is the wrong choice of words. But they're good peeps."

"Okay."

"You'll really like Sarah when you meet her. Ethan's girl. She's the sweetest broad you're ever gonna come across. I can't stand the awful way people treat her, because I don't think she's ever had a bad thought about anybody in her entire life. Even people who deserved it, eh. As for me, I've dreamed up all kinds of horrible stuff in my darker moments. And the guys, well, *they're guys.*"

Dya nodded. She knew exactly what Molly meant.

"I've just been busy," Dya said, which was also a dodge. She was simply too gun shy to just walk up to someone and strike up a conversation, no matter who they were. *What would I say?!*

"Whatever suits ya, girlie," Molly said with a shrug. "I've told them all about you. They wanna meet you for sure."

"When you come back."

"Wicked." Molly palm-muted a hard, staccato riff on her guitar. "This is something new I'm working on. I want you to sing on it."

"I am at your service."

"How'd you like those CDs?"

"They're fantastic! I cannot stop playing them."

"Ha ha! Bet your grandma just loves that, eh!"

"She doesn't mind," Dya said. "She is very cool. She prefers the singing over the screaming, but it's all great."

"Yuh, you gotta have the mix," Molly said, now absently finger-picking a dark, melancholy melody. "It's the interplay of soft and hard, light and heavy that's best. That's art. That's *life*, you know it?"

"That's deep."

They laughed.

"Here, can you sing this line?"

Molly played the dark melody again.

"What do you want me to sing?"

"Just ooooos or aaaaahs or something. Words will come later, I just wanna hear it out loud for now."

"Do you want a harmony?"

"Sure, if you can."

Dya began to sing, following the note pattern Molly plucked. In an effort to mask her "sea voice," she tried her best to imitate the rounder, more obtuse singing she was familiar with from listening to the radio. Careful to sing just one melodic line at a time. Molly smiled and nodded in approval.

But suddenly, and for just a brief moment, Dya's voice slipped. Accidentally. In an instant, a richer, more subaqueous tone resonated from Dya's throat, harmonic with the standard notes…but utterly alien to Molly's ears. The quick sound was *layered*, nearly polytonal, complete with sympathetic notes. Molly shivered and gasped, her eyes wide in disbelief. Dya shut her mouth quickly.

Oops…

"Whoa, dude…" Molly whispered, momentarily stunned. Dya's cheeks flushed pink.

Just then, Molly's phone chimed from the floor beside the couch. She snapped back to reality, sure that the gorgeous, otherworldly sound she'd heard had just been her imagination. "Could you get that, Dya?"

Dya reached down and retrieved the phone.

Beep.

"Hello?"

"Uh…Moll?"

"No, but would you like to speak with her?"

"This must be Dya," Malik said.

"It must be," Dya replied, her cheeks warming to pink again.

"What's good, girl?"

"Um, everything I guess," Dya stammered. "What's, uh, good with you, Malik?"

"You know. Livin' the dream. It's what I do."

She giggled and said, "Here's Molly," quickly passing the phone off.

"What up, homie," Molly said into the phone. "Yup. No, we're just hangin', eh, working on some music. Yuh. Yuh, it's wicked. What? Okay, I'll see." Molly looked toward Dya and asked, "You wanna grab a pizza, Dy?"

"Thanks, but I have to get home," Dya replied. "Mary Louise freaks out if I'm gone too long. She thinks I'm going to get snatched off the street or something."

Molly chuckled and shook her head, then said into the phone, "No dice. Okay, I'll see you in a bit, babe. Okay, later," and hung up. "Who the hell's gonna snatch you off the street, eh? Just lay the screech on 'em like you did Jimmie Kendall, right? Problem solved."

If only you knew...

"Rain check for sure," Dya said. "What's Malik up to?"

"Detention. For the skipping," Molly said. "He just got out. Apparently, even though I got suspended for 'fighting,' nobody else got suspended for it as well. What the hell do they think happened? Did I fight my own damn self or something?"

"That sucks," Dya said. "It sucks a lot."

"Forget what I said before, eh. *That's* life."

"And it sucks."

"What can you do."

"What are you and Malik doing tonight?"

"We're gonna play at his place for a bit."

"You're gonna *play*?" Dya asked with a wink and a grin.

"Make a little beautiful music together, you know?" Molly said, returning the smile. "Seriously, though, just practice pads and acoustic guitar. We do it all the time. We're gonna start playing at Sarah's place, and Ethan's gonna play bass, but we haven't gotten that far yet."

"Is Ethan any good?"

"Mal's played with him. Says he has potential if he really woodsheds."

"I think it's awesome that you and Malik have that to share. It's romantic...in, you know, a metal sort of way."

"What can I say, eh," Molly said with an affected sigh. "I'm a lucky girl. Mal is a *sick-ass* drummer. On top of being a sugar-muffin. We're gonna be legendary. Someday."

"You guys could be the heavy metal Captain and Tennille."

"I don't know who that is."

"Yeah. Me neither."

Always Careful

Over the next five years I spent nearly half of my time on land. At first I would return to the sea every night, then every other day, then a few times a week, and so on. Every so often checking in with my people down in the hollows. Always finding it thoroughly unchanged, and myself unmissed. All was going well, and I had no real cause for concern (for a while). And there was simply too much fun to be had.

She would sneak me in through her window in the middle of the night. Of course I was always careful only to whisper unless Mary Louise was left home alone (which she more frequently was as time went on). I wasn't supposed to be there. I did not yet exist.

When we were alone we would dance for hours, Mary Louise and I, to rock-and-roll and rhythm-and-blues records her brother in the army brought home for her—Little Richard, Big Joe Turner, Fats Domino. Some others like Bill Haley, who were just okay. Nothing special. Our favorite, however, was Elmore James. We would sing at the top of our little, girly voices—

"She said, Baaaaaaaaay-beeeee baby baby baby pleeeeeease come back to meeeeeeee / You know I love you baby / And you know all your love is freeeee..."

And, of course, I shared songs from the deep with her, which she grew to love with such intensity that it rather frightened me.

THE SONG IN THE SQUALL

I believe they are known as 'siren songs' in land folklore, and here I witnessed their power firsthand. I knew I had to be careful with those songs in particular, for the sake of my friend, and anyone else who might hear them. They are beautiful. And they are dangerous. Much like my people themselves.

I would often try to avoid singing certain pieces, unless Mary Louise was particularly adamant about hearing them. Or if she was suffering one of her frequent headaches. Then I would do anything she asked. I would gently rub her temples with my fingertips and sing a deep-sea lullaby. It seemed to be the only remedy that would help at all.

"I wish I could teach you how to heal yourself like I can," I told her. "A headache should be such a simple thing to push from you. Won't you give it a try?"

"I'll be okay," she would say, her eyes shut tight in agony. "It just takes time. Just time, that's all."

I've never understood that. I likely never will.

A Circle of Friends

"Just let me go!" Dya cried, tears burning her lightly freckled cheeks. "I didn't do anything to any of you!"

Click click click click.

"Ooooo, that shot was perfect, Trina! Her lips are all pouty and everything."

Trina Beckett and three of her friends had Dya cornered in the handicapped stall of the girls bathroom, snapping pictures of her with their camera phones.

"This one is definitely going on the site," Trina laughed. "Do you know about the website, slut? It's just the best. You'll love it."

"I don't know what you're talking about!" Dya cried harder. She knew she could probably scream all four of them right through the wall if she'd wanted to. But there would be no explaining that away. So she had to endure this.

"We'll call it: *Dya's Mouth: Open For Business*!"

"*First Come First to Come*!" another girl squealed, and they all shrieked with laughter. "Bet your ugly little dyke girlfriend Molly Jones knows ALL about that, eh!"

"Please! I'm"—*sob*—"late for c-class!"

"Oh, I'm sooooorry," Trina replied in a mocking tone. "Why didn't you say so?" The four girls parted to give her a clear exit. Dya tried to run past them, but a clandestine foot sent her stumbling to the floor.

THE SONG IN THE SQUALL

"Jesus! *Ha ha!* Walk much, retard?"

Dya jumped up quickly, righted herself and headed out the bathroom door, and away from their peals of grating cackles.

"Hey!" the hall monitor shouted at Dya as she ran past. "No running, eh!"

"So nice of you to join us," Mr. Barkley, the photography teacher, said in a drab monotone as Dya ran into the lab ten minutes late, her eyes and cheeks still blotchy red. "I suggest you get cracking immediately. Like, yesterday."

Because she had no partner, and no effort had been made to assign her to a new team, Dya was already behind. Her shoulders fell, resigned to her fate and sat down at her table alone.

"Excuse me, Mr. Barkley?" Molly said.

"What is it now, Miss Jones?" the teacher sighed.

"Seeing as how Dya doesn't have a partner, and my partner is a total douche hose—"

"*Suck it, Columbine,*" Molly's assigned partner Joey LaDue growled at her under his breath.

"You want to switch partners, I have no objection," Barkley replied, not bothering to look up from his issue of *Field & Stream*. "Do you object, Mr. LaDue?"

"She was a drag on me anyway, Mr. Barkley."

"Wonderful. Then we're all happy."

Molly plopped her enormous army surplus backpack down on Dya's table and grinned. Dya smiled back, grateful once again.

"We're eating lunch outside this week, eh," Molly whispered. "Rain or shine."

"Is that an invitation?" Dya whispered back.

"Well duuuuuh."

"I'll come tomorrow."

"Wicked."

* * *

"Great to finally meet you, Dya!" Sarah said, embracing Dya warmly. "Sorry to invade your personal space. I hug everybody. I'm a big hugger."

"That she is," Ethan, Malik and Molly said, more or less in unison.

"I don't mind," Dya said, wrapping her arms around the bigger girl and returning the hug, not bothered a bit by the poke of Sarah's nickel-studded dog collar against her shoulder blade.

The five of them sat out on the front steps of school eating their lunches, enjoying the autumn chill. The sky was gray and overcast, and threatening rain. Just the sort of atmosphere that suited them.

*The moisture in the air...*Dya thought...*it's so delicious...*

"So...you're pretty infamous 'round these old corridors, eh," Sarah said to Dya. "Well played, madam. Well played."

She was, of course, referring to the incident of Jimmie in the darkroom (and Jimmie's subsequent "expulsion"), and not the situation on the field. Only Dya, Molly, and Jimmie knew of that, and they weren't talking in detail.

"Well," Dya said with a dismissive little shrug, "you can't believe everything you read in the British tabloids."

Everyone laughed, and Dya gave a little inner sigh of relief. She'd heard that line on some stupid TV show, and the audience had laughed at it as well. She was glad it yielded the same response for her; though she was pretty sure she hadn't gotten it quite right.

"So you gonna jam with us?" Ethan asked Dya, his mouth packed with sandwich once again. "We could use a vocalist, and buzz is that you don't exactly suck."

"If you'd like me to, absolutely," Dya said. "But, you know, Molly can sing. She has a really pretty voice."

"Pretty ain't enough for what we're laying down, sister," Molly said. "It's gotta *rage*."

"And with alla her fancy finger work," Ethan said, "Moll can't be distracted by vocal duties on top, eh."

"You a fan of the Baroness EP?" Malik asked.

"I most certainly am," Dya replied. *As of a few days ago…*

"Then you're hired!"

"So all of you play?" Dya asked, munching her pineapple and kiwi.

"Been hitting the skins since I was nine years old," said Malik. "Where I'm from, if you can't ball, you might as well be prancing around in pink-laced panties. But because of my jacked-up leg, sports were a no-go. So I just hid inside with the drums."

"And now we all reap the sweet fruits of your childhood trauma," said Ethan. "Seems fair to me."

"I've been playing about seven years too," Molly said. "Give or take."

"I'm practicing my bass every day," said Ethan sheepishly. "But I've got some catching up to do with these two, eh."

"Hey man," Malik said to Ethan, "it's not like you're, you know, *terrible* or anything."

"Thanks Mal," Ethan replied, deadpan. "Your encouragement warms the very cockles of my heart."

"Not quite about your cockles, dog," Malik replied. "But you know I'm here for ya."

"I don't play at all," Sarah said, resting her head on Ethan's shoulder. "I'm just a bass groupie."

"Don't listen to her, Dya," Malik said. "Sare's a video designer."

"A *wannabe* video designer," Sarah clarified.

"Whatever, girl," Malik said. "We're *all* wannabes."

Too true, Dya thought to herself.

Thunder rumbled in the distance, and a number of folks headed back inside the school.

"Sarah's designing a killer video to project on stage while we perform," Molly said. "That is…if we ever actually get a gig and all."

"That sounds terrific," Dya said, although truthfully she had no idea of what they were talking about.

The rain that had been spitting and dribbling throughout most of the lunch period finally gave way and began to shower down. The few other students left eating their lunches on the front steps scurried off inside. But not these five. They simply pulled their hoods up over their heads and sat, soaking it all in.

Ethan growled in an affected gruff bellow, his hands playing an invisible bass guitar.

"*A dark raaaain / in Portland, Maaaaine...uh...something something death and pain...*"

"Needs work, brother," said Malik.

"It'll sound better in 6/8, eh."

Ignoring her friends' chatter, Molly stood up and held out her arms. So taken was she with the feel of the cold rain, she leaned her head back, letting the water splash against her bare face.

"God, this feels so good," she said, smiling wide to catch the droplets in her mouth.

"You're such a freak, Moll," Sarah laughed, cuddling close to Ethan. "But that's why we love you."

But that's why we love you, Dya repeated silently to herself. *I like that. I like that a lot.*

October came upon greater Portland and exploded in a dazzling blast of gold, crimson, and blood orange. The maple and birch blazed defiantly in the sunlight against the encroaching, and inevitable, gnash of winter. Never before had Dya seen anything quite so beautiful.

Coral has nothing on this!

The days grew shorter, the evenings darker, and ever more they became inseparable. The five of them. Dya's new little circle of friends. And, at last, she felt as if she truly, completely belonged on land.

* * *

THE SONG IN THE SQUALL

"You're gonna dig these cats, Dy," Sarah said as they all piled into Malik's sister's car. "They are wicked sick. I hope you're wearing your dancing shoes, eh."

Dya's first local concert was a truly momentous occasion, though she could not remember the names of any of the bands. The joint was packed. Probably over capacity. The music was so loud it was hard to tell what the musicians were actually playing. But she didn't care.

The 'dancing' here primarily consisted of jumping up and down and slamming into one another. There appeared to be no rhyme, reason or rhythm to any of it. None that Dya could perceive. *I suppose that's what makes it great.* Ethan and Malik grabbed each other's arms and swung around like a human top, knocking people down in the process. Dya was sure that she had never laughed so hard in her life.

Deep into the set, the final band of the night tried their hands at a cover of High On Fire's "Hung, Drawn, and Quartered." It was a marginal success at best, but the place went nuts all the same. Dya and her friends cheered wildly.

"I know this song!" Dya screamed, holding up her fingers in the devil horns.

When the galloping drums exploded, bodies flew into one another with reckless abandon. Caught up in the spirit of it all, Dya climbed up onto the stage as she had seen others do, and dove off into the crowd's waiting hands. It was great fun...and it made no sense at all. *But who cares about sense?!*

Falling back into the pocket of the crowd where her friends were, they all threw their arms around one another as they sang, screamed and growled the cryptic lyrics in unison. And as Dya belted out, *"The evil has come and the darkness will cover the light / above the legions, who will slay the poor and the bliiiiiind!!!"* she nearly drowned out the band itself. Malik, Ethan, and Sarah couldn't help but stare, slack-jawed and gob-smacked by the power of her voice. Ditto many others in their immediate vicinity.

"I told you guys!" Molly yelled to them over the band's squealing feedback and the roar of the crowd, laughing at their collective bafflement, "Didn't I tell you about her, eh? Whatever it is, my girl's *got* it!"

Dya just smiled and shrugged. "It's just something I can do, you know?"

For the most part, the lot of them never really got up to much, but for "bumming around town" as Ethan called it. They'd check out the few independent record shops and alternative bookstores that still existed. Otherwise they would lounge about watching the Brian DePalma adaptation of Stephen King's *Carrie* over and over on an old, murky VHS tape.

"That girl is one of us, you know?"

"Get 'em, Carrie! Squash 'em good!"

They could usually be seen just hanging out on the flat rocks by the sea for hours on end, talking away, as the churning water crashed close by.

This was a trial for Dya, of course, the cool mist and salt spray on the breeze teasing her lips and tongue. It was painful, to be so close and not even so much as touch it. It physically hurt. The waves beckoned to her. Taunted her...

"Theoretical question, eh," Ethan said. "If you could live anywhere...anywhere in the world...where would it be?"

"Somewhere hot," Sarah replied, shivering.

"I've lived somewhere hot, Sare," Malik said. "Trust me when I tell you that it blows."

"Okay, what about you, Mal?"

"Nowhere specific. Nowhere set. I'd wanna live on the road. Always on tour."

"That's my baby," Molly said, shoulder-deep in the lapping waves. "I could co-sign on that plan, eh."

...It didn't help matters either that Molly would invariably wade into the water, if not dive in head on. Dya was sick with envy to watch her swim, though not resentful. *How can I blame her? I would do it too if I could.*

"So how about you, Molly?"

"What, where would I live if I could?"

"Yuh."

"Somewhere far from here, I know that much. But somewhere cold. Colder than here."

"Colder than here?!?"

"Yuh. Somewhere eternally cold, dark and…I don't know, eh…somethin'."

Endless? Dya thought. Been there. Trust me when I tell you…and so on.

"Yeesh," Ethan said, his eyes a-roll. "Okay, Moll, you win the 'most metal' award for the day, eh."

"I gotta be me."

In time, Dya's craving for the sea did diminish, if only slightly. She resisted the temptation. And felt, for the time, that she was stronger overall for the resistance.

"All right, Dy, your turn."

"Right here."

"What? What do you mean?"

"This is where I would live if I could. Right here. Forever."

"Really? Here? Huh. Wow. Okay. Takes all kinds, I guess."

October soldiered on. Winter loomed, nearer by the day. Life at school was no better than it had been. Other students, for their part, pretended Dya did not exist, but to occasionally push her out of the way, regardless of how fast she walked down the hall. And she had grown well accustomed to seeing "DYA = DIRTY SLUT" written in black sharpie on the walls of the girls' washroom. It was probably in the boys' room as well. She was sure of it.

* * *

It was a cold, wet Friday. Dya stood waiting for her after-school bus in bare feet, her shoes in her backpack to keep them dry. She minded neither the cold nor the pouring rain. It was her kind of day. Still, she wasn't going to turn down a ride.

"Yo, Dya!"

From under the hood of her sopping wet sweatshirt she looked out across the street to see Malik waving her over from inside his sister's car. She ran over to him, splashing through near-freezing puddles.

"Hey, Mal," she said, sliding into the empty passenger seat. "Where's Molly? She wasn't in sixth bell."

"She went home early," he said, easing out into traffic. "Headache or something."

"Really? That's weird. She is *never* sick I thought."

"She's sick of school."

"Ah."

"Yeah..."

"Did...something happen?"

"I don't know the details," he said, turning down the God Forbid CD playing on the stereo, "but apparently somebody in her third bell was talking smack about her brother today. Like, real loud, in front of everybody. She's...yeah. She's pretty upset."

"Oh god. Her brother who died?"

"No, the one in the joint. The middle one. Charles. Guess he was kinda 'the man' at this school about a decade ago...well before he started stealing cars and robbing houses. And this somebody in Molly's third period thought the whole mess was just a laugh riot. Molly, it seems, did not concur."

"Oh no."

"That's how it goes sometimes."

"Poor Molly. I should call her when I get home."

"I wouldn't."

"Why not?"

"Well...Molly doesn't keep secrets, and she'll tell you about it if you ask. But she doesn't like to talk about Charles. It's humiliating for her, I suppose. I mean, I personally don't think it's that big of a deal. I've got family in the pen myself. But he was her hero. Guess he kinda fell off when their moms passed, but Molly's rose-colored Charlie glasses wouldn't let her see it."

"Her eyes aren't that good anyway."

"True enough. Charles walked on water as far as she was concerned. And when he fell short of the glory, and she had to face up to the reality of what he had done…let's just say it broke her heart. Folks aren't always who you think they are, you know?"

"I do," Dya said, casting her gaze out the rain-streaked window glass. "I do know that for sure."

There was a lull in the conversation as they drove on, listening to the rain patter against the car. Suddenly, Malik said, "We need a weekend out," as if it had just hit him. "All of us. Clear out the mental poison. You know? It'd be good for us."

"What do you mean?"

"I don't know; we just need to get out. Before the Maine winter unleashes its beat-down upon Portland—"

"It's *wicked* beat-down, remember."

They laughed.

"You're right," Malik said, pulling onto Dya's street. "Gotta come correct with the Maine-ese. Before winter unleashes its *wicked* beat-down upon Portland, a serious camping trip is in order for sure. I've got all my granddad's gear just gathering dust. Now's the time."

"I've never been camping," Dya said.

"What?! Naaaw."

"I haven't. My family was never into that sort of thing."

"For real? Not once?"

"Seriously. For real. Never have."

"Well that cinches the deal then. We gotta get our camp on with the quickness."

"Sounds like fun to me."

"It'll be dope for sure. Spread the word."

"I'll alert the troops," Dya said opening the passenger-side door. Though only late afternoon, the sky above was as dark as night. "Thanks for the ride, Mal."

"Hold on a sec," he said, and jumped out on his side. Reaching into the backseat right behind the driver's side, Malik grabbed an umbrella and ran around to Dya's side.

"You don't have to do that," she said, stepping out into the teeming rain, nearly shin-deep in water. "I don't mind getting wet."

"Girl, please," Malik said, holding the umbrella over Dya's head and putting his arm around her shoulder. "If my granddad knew I'd shirked my gentlemanly duties and let a lady walk from my car in the rain he'd drag himself outta his deathbed just to light my ass up."

"Well thanks," she said. They walked side-by-side to the front door of her apartment complex. Once there, she leaned up on tiptoes to give him a hug goodbye. "And thanks again for the ride."

"Any time," he said, hugging her back.

The embrace lasted just a tiny bit longer than normal. Perhaps a tiny bit longer that it should have. But not too much.

"I'll see you this weekend I'm sure," Malik said, turning to go. "Tell Mary Louise I said 'hey.'"

"I will." Pause. "Hey, Malik?"

"Yeah?"

"You want to maybe come in for a little while? Just until the storm eases up."

He stood in the rain for a moment, and Dya could tell he was mulling it over.

Finally he said, "Nah, I'd better not. I think Pops is cooking, so I should prolly get home." He turned to limp back to the car.

"Suit yourself. Night, Mal."

"Good night, m'lady," he said, and slid awkwardly into the driver's seat. And as he drove off, Dya could once again not shake the *déjà vu*.

I've heard that before...

The More I Began To Change

It was in this fourth full year of our friendship that something which should have been obvious to us well before became truly apparent—Mary Louise and I, by all appearances...were aging at the same rate. Starting at age "ten" we remained, by any observable standard, the same age as one another year after year.

It was she who noticed this, much to her delight. I, however, was horrified. Because, of course, this meant that I was aging at an extremely accelerated rate from what would have been normal for me. How on earth would I keep this obvious physical change from my people in the deep?!

"Perhaps they won't notice?" she suggested.

"Yes, yes, that's possible," I replied, grasping at the comforting straws. "They are practically oblivious to my existence anyway."

"Well then there you go. No need to freak yourself out over nothing."

Nothing?! How could this be nothing?!?!

"Yes," I said. "Perhaps I am panicking for no reason." I truly wanted to believe this.

"Just try not to worry, Dya," she said. "I suspect that everything will be just fine. They won't notice."

I hope. I hope...

They did notice, however. How could they not? And it was not "just fine" in the slightest. Not in the deep. It was instead quite an unpleasant scene. Much to-do was made about the disgrace I had brought to my family's good name. Idle threats of what would surely happen when my parents returned, as if there was any chance of them ever actually coming back.

—You might as well be killing yourself—snarled my uncle Kalae.—In fact, that is precisely what you are doing—

—And what if you were seen, Dya—my aunt Traydla said, piling further on.—You know full well you could be putting us all in danger—

I was forbidden from ever returning to land. I was required to always clear my travel with Kalae, whose sense of my whereabouts was often cloudy. (This had something to do with "damage" he had acquired long, long ago, but I was not allowed to ask about it. Surprise, surprise.)

So, I did as I was told...

For a while.

Then I was ignored again.

And away I went...

Although we initially took pains to keep me in sunglasses and my shiny, silver hair tied up under a sunhat to avoid people on the street noticing my more...exotic features, I must admit that after a time we began to grow rather lax about not flaunting my "otherness" in public. There was something of a kick about the second glances people would toss me. I was, I suppose, different enough to notice...but not quite freakish enough to cause a panic.

Mary Louise and I would stroll through town heads high and chatting away, feigning casual oblivion. Then, once we were alone, we would fall to pieces in a fit of giggles over all the goggle-eyed gawking.

It was stupid. And foolish. And careless. And even kind of reckless. And so much fun.

These efforts at concealment, thin though they were, ultimately turned out to be unnecessary. For as we discovered, the longer I

stayed out of the ocean, the more I began to change. The silver of my hair darkened to a deep auburn. My nails grew clear. My skin took on a freckled, peachy hue. The sharpness of my face softened. My eyes faded to hazel.
   "Well, you're just a regular girl now."
   "Don't sound so disappointed, Mary Louise!"
   "I'm not! It's just...I don't know."
   I certainly wasn't disappointed anyway. I could not have been happier. Not only could I pass...I was thoroughly, utterly unremarkable!

"Mary Louise," her mother asked, "who is your lovely friend?"
   "Mom," fourteen-year-old Mary Louise replied, "this is Dya...Dya Schmidt. Her parents are Bill and Francine Schmidt. You, uh, remember them, right? They vacation here sometimes."
   "Hmmm...yes I think I do. How do you do, Dya?"
   "Very well ma'am, thank you."
   "Will you be staying the whole summer?"
   "I certainly hope to, yes. But, sadly, probably not. I love it here. It just depends upon my father's work schedule."
   "My, what a beautiful name. Is it Greek?"
   "Schmidt?"
   "We would love to have you and your parents over for dinner sometime."
   "That would be wonderful, ma'am. I'll ask them straight away."
   "I remember Bill Schmidt," Mary Louise's father chimed in from the kitchen, a wooden pipe in his teeth.
   Uh oh...
   "Yes, sir?"
   "Didn't know he had a daughter."
   "Two, actually. My sis's away at college."
   I am really pushing it now...
   "So, how is the old lad?"
   "Oh, you know daddy," I said. "Same as he ever was, sir."

"How did that merger of his go? With that Italian firm?"

"Hal," his wife said, exasperated, "don't pester the poor girl with such things."

"Yes, yes. Fine." He returned to his newspaper with a hearty chuckle at the funny pages.

"It was lovely to meet you, Dya. I hope to see you around a lot this summer, however long you may be staying."

"Thank you, ma'am. You surely will."

"You two run off and have fun," she said to Mary Louise and me. And so we did.

Needless to say, the dinner never took place. Along with the rapid pace and perpetual impermanence, it seems that adult-onset chronic forgetfulness is a common condition of life on land. Come to think of it, it is in the deep as well.

A Song Just For Us

"Now be sure to layer up when the sun sets," Mary Louise said to Dya as they packed her overnight duffel. "There are few colder places in the world than a Maine forest at night."

"Mary Louise," Dya laughed, "I'm pretty sure *I can handle the cold!*"

Mary Louise chuckled as well at the realization.

"Yeah, I suppose you can," she said. "But still…best to be safe."

Dya sighed and threw in an extra pair of heavy wool socks and an additional fleece jacket.

"I wish you would come with us," Dya said.

"Oh come now," said Mary Louise dismissively.

"You should!"

"That's ridiculous."

"They're all crazy about you."

True enough. Ethan, Sarah, Molly, and Malik were very fond of Mary Louise indeed. And, but for "band practice" days (which at this stage consisted mostly of fooling around and making a disorganized racket), Dya and Mary Louise's apartment was quickly becoming their hang out of choice. The all-but-absolute freedom they had there was likely a contributing factor.

"That's very sweet," replied Mary Louise.

"Do you know what they all say?"

"What do they say?"

"They all say, 'We wish *our* grandmas were as wicked cool as yours, eh!'"

They both laughed heartily.

"Well, I like them too," Mary Louise said, still chuckling. "They're good kids. I'm glad you met them."

"The invitation stands," said Dya, sing-song.

"My camping days are over, love. I like my roof overhead, and my couch, and my central heating, thank you very much all the same."

"I'll miss you," Dya said.

She meant to say it in a joking way, but that's not how it sounded coming out of her mouth. And it was true. After fifty-one years apart, the thought of not seeing her friend for two whole days was suddenly a rather difficult pill to swallow, excited as she was for the short excursion.

Mary Louise smiled and touched Dya's face.

"You have fun with your friends," she said.

"I will."

They finished packing.

"School's better these days, yeah?"

"It's as terrible as always," Dya replied with an affected groan. "But...when people say things, now I just laugh. It doesn't matter."

"A pretty girl like you?" Mary Louise said, incredulous. "What could they *possibly* say about you?"

"The latest is: The reason Jimmie Kendall is no longer at school is because I apparently infected him with AIDS. I don't even know what that is. What is it?"

"Never mind," said Mary Louise, waving it off.

"And, of course, they still call me names."

"Like what?"

"Like Columbine."

"Oh, Jesus..."

"I don't even understand it," Dya said. "I mean; I know what it means. But I don't know what it has to do with me."

"That is…I'm sorry…that is just awfully stupid."

"Yes. Exactly."

"All because of that incident with Judge Kendall's boy."

"I suppose."

"That wasn't your doing, love. That little punk needs therapy. If anyone is dangerous, it's him. Not you."

"But people thought he was *cool*," Dya said. "And I'm this nobody. And he got in trouble and I'm to blame."

"I've never understood how jerks can be popular. That has always seemed a contradiction to me."

"It's because they are *selectively* jerky. They're just fine to everybody who isn't…us."

"Well…none of that matters now, right?"

"No, it doesn't matter that everybody thinks I'm either a diseased tramp or some sort of freak."

"Don't let it bother you."

"I don't."

"This isn't the deep, honey," Mary Louise said. "Social mores are different up here. Maybe they shouldn't be. But they are."

"I know."

"You okay?"

"I'm okay."

"Columbine…" Mary Louise chuckled, shaking her head.

"It's still better than what they called me at first," said Dya.

"What," Mary Louise said with a small grin, "*the new fish?*"

"It's so disgusting."

"Believe it or not, sweetheart, *it's nothing personal*. That's what everyone is called when they're new. Even in my day."

"It doesn't matter what they say," repeated Dya with a shrug, as if to convince herself.

"Now there's a good life lesson," Mary Louise said. "See, this school thing was a good idea after all. You learn more in the hallways than you do in the classroom sometimes."

"I just don't understand the point of it," said Dya. "All the pettiness and cruelty. And it's not just the students either. It's the teachers too. They're just as bad in some ways. What's the use?"

"You'll understand when you're older."

"Ha ha very funny."

"Well it does serve you right," Mary Louise said, "you are pretty much a world-class floozy."

"That's what I mean," Dya said. "If I'm going to be branded a slut or some such, shouldn't I at least get to earn it?"

"Welcome to another great life lesson, hon."

"I should certainly have high marks this term."

"Just remember," Mary Louise said, a bit more seriously, "you have the *power* in the end. Right? You have the advantage. You can do things that no one else up here can do."

"No," Dya said insistently, "I can't. I'm just a normal, average girl. Remember?"

"Uh huh. Of course you are."

"I am."

"And you have really great friends," Mary Louise said. "And you have me."

She smiled at Mary Louise.

You really are beautiful, Dya thought.

"All right," Mary Louise said, back to business, "you all set here?"

Dya struggled to zip up her overstuffed duffel. With some effort, she finally succeeded.

"I think I'm all ready. Malik's driving, and he says he knows just the spot. He's borrowing his sister's car for the weekend."

"I thought Malik only had his temps," said Mary Louise. Dya gave her a look that said, *You're not really my grandmother, remember?* Mary Louise held up a defensive palm.

"I'm just saying," she replied to the look. "Hey, I trust Malik. He seems very responsible." She paused for a moment, looking off, her forehead scrunched up in thought. "Something about that boy, though..."

"What?" Dya asked. "What about him?"

"Oh, it's nothing bad. It's just...the first time they all came over, your little crew...the first time I met them...he just seemed...familiar to me somehow."

"You've probably just seen him out on the street somewhere. Portland's big, but it isn't all that big."

"No...it's nothing like that," Mary Louise said. "It's something about his eyes. And the shape of his chin."

"The shape of his chin? What on earth are you talking about?"

"I don't know," said Mary Louise. "Probably just my senility slipping in a shade early."

"Well, won't that be a treat for us all."

"I'm looking forward to it."

The downstairs buzzer sounded.

"That's them," Dya said, throwing her bag over her shoulder. She kissed Mary Louise on the cheek and bounced out the door. "Love you."

"Love you too."

"Come on, you guys!" Malik shouted through the trees. "It's up this way!"

He loped on ahead as the rest tried to keep up. Despite having an awkward gait caused by a left leg some inches longer than the right, Malik was surprisingly fast on his feet when he wanted to be. Sarah, Ethan and Molly trailed behind, huffing and puffing, their backpacks bobbing and bouncing against their backs. Dya ran right behind them, pretending to be winded as well.

"Good lord, Mal," Ethan gasped, "this s-spot...bet...better...be worth it, eh."

Dya had to resist stopping to gape at the vibrant color bursting from the trees all around. She could have stared at them all day, but didn't want to fall behind and get lost. She could not yet sense when they were not nearby. And she suspected that she never would be able to.

Perhaps you can't do that at all anymore...

She was frightened, and perhaps a bit thrilled, by the thought that that might just be true. *One small step closer to permanence.* She could still feel Mary Louise, however. And her people far off in the sea. But the latter was fading, thinner and thinner by the day.

As Molly, Sarah, Ethan, and Dya entered a clearing, they found Malik standing right in the center of a grouping of maples, the sunshine pouring down upon him, and a perfect spot of flat ground. He extended both arms to each side, grinning a mile wide.

"Did I not say this is *the* spot? I thought you *knew* your boy could camp, son!"

Ethan built the fire as the girls helped Malik put up the tent.
"This was my granddad Marvin's tent," Malik said.
Dya gulped.
No, no, Dya thought to herself. *It's a common name I'm sure.* She tried her best not to study his eyes. Or the shape of his chin.
"Left over from his military days," Malik continued as they pounded the stakes into the solid, near-frozen earth. "Old man forgets nothing, loses nothing, throws nothing away. In this rare case, that's a positive. It'll keep out everything: cold, rain, wind, bears, Sasquatch, terrorists, you name it." The green canvas rippled in the breeze. "Downside, though," he said, "it does smell like an old, burlap sack."

Can't be...It just can't be...

That night, after dinner, they sat around Ethan's fire, just chatting away about anything and everything, as they were wont to do: school, movies, "the band," which was mostly still just an idea at this point. Molly absently strummed minor chords on her acoustic guitar, occasionally needing to warm her stiff fingers over the burning logs.

"This fire's wicked good, baby," Sarah said to Ethan. They snuggled close, sharing a large blue comforter with the image of a giant wolf's head sewn in. Malik sat with his arm around Molly as she played the guitar, absently patting out rhythms on his thigh. "How'd you get so multi-talented?"

"You can thank the scouts, eh," said Ethan.

"You don't strike me as the scouts type, dude," Molly said, not looking up from her instrument.

"Oh, it was brief," Ethan said, with a thin chuckle. "I didn't last long at all. The other guys made it pretty clear that they didn't want me there. Their dads didn't seem to like me much either. I took the hint and hit the bricks. Pops called me a 'no-good quitter.' But hey, I kept the manual. It comes in handy, eh. We let this fire burn all night, we'll have some wicked coals for pancakes in the morning."

Molly began to sing along to the chords she was strumming. It was a song Dya knew well from Mary Louise's radio.

"*Yes'n I try to ignore / All this blood on the floor / It's just this heart on my sleeve that is bleeding...*"

"God, I love this song," Sarah said, her eyes closed and head swaying back and forth. "Ray LaMontagne is such the hotness."

"He's my favoritest music in the world right now," Molly said, continuing to play, "right after Mastodon."

She sang—

"*Oh so kiss him again / just to prove that you can / and I will stand here and burn in my skin...*"

When Molly finished, they all clapped.

"Thank you, thank you. Be sure to tip your bartenders."

"For a raging metal demon, Moll," Ethan said, "you ain't half bad at the sensitive-folkie thing."

"It's the yin and the yang, dude," Molly said.

"For real."

"You know," Dya said, "Ray LaMontagne is a Mainer. He lives not too far from where a friend of Mary Louise's used to live. Her neighbor told her that she saw him at the Home Depot buying pine mulch."

"I've heard variations of that story from so many people, eh," Ethan said. "That dude must have the mulchiest property in all of Maine."

They laughed and laughed.

"So who knows a story?" Malik asked. "Anybody? Preferably something with murderers and pick axes and stuff."

"Howzbout you, Dy?" Ethan said.

"Howzbout me what?"

"I'll bet you've got something you've been holdin' out on us."

"Like what?"

"Like anything, eh. From the *old country*, or wherever in hell you're from. You're all mysterious and junk."

"Nah dude," Dya said, trying to sound like Molly. It was clumsy and self-conscious. "No stories or anything."

Don't do that anymore...

"Come oooooon," Ethan pressed further. The rest chimed in likewise. Dya felt pulled like a tightrope.

"I don't know," Dya said.

I just don't know.

"Look, Dy," Sarah said, "something you should know. We're *all* outsiders here, eh."

Well obviously...

"That's right, girl," Malik said. "Maine's a beautiful state, but if your family doesn't have roots spreading down nine generations into the ground, you're a newbie. A tourist. And not too welcome."

"It's not really that bad in Portland," Molly offered. "But man, out in the sticks you'll be shunned for just moving away for a while and then coming back."

"When my grandmamma died," Malik said, "my dad moved us up here from Huntsville. I was small then. Granddad came up to live with us a couple of years ago. Claimed he had come up here briefly when he was a teenager and always wanted to get back. But hell, I don't know if that's even true."

"Pretty much same deal for Ethan and me," said Molly. "Our dads came up for the lobster boats."

"From where?" Dya asked.

"From away."

"Pops didn't last too long on the boat, eh," said Ethan. "Sarah's the only one of us who goes back three generations."

"And that's not near long enough," Sarah interjected. "I might as well be a tourist. So don't worry, Dya. You're truly among fellow misfits. Not just at school, but *everywhere*."

The back of Dya's neck prickled. She did want to share more with them. But how much *could* she tell? How much could she really trust?

Would they understand? Would they be scared? Worst of all...what if they ask too many questions?

"Molly," Dya said, finally. "Play those chords again. The ones you were playing before. But pluck them with your fingertips instead."

"Yuh, okay."

Molly began to pick through a simple, dark progression.

"Slow it down a little more please."

She did.

"Switch the second chord with the third and vice versa."

"Um...You got it. I think."

Dya closed her eyes, found the pitch in her throat, and began to sing for them. An ancient song. One from the deep. One she had been taught when she was very young. She did not bother to translate it to English...but it didn't matter. It was a folk song, after all. It lived less in the words, but in the tones—

A girl from the deep and a young sailor out to sea fall in love. Every night, he sneaks from his cabin and dives into the water to be with her. They want to be together forever, but cannot find the way. One night, a furious squall whips up from nowhere, sending the ship crashing back and forth. The sailors desperately try to batten down the hatches, but chances of survival look ever more bleak. Suddenly, over the deafening wind and thunderous, crashing waves, the young sailor hears the voice of his love singing for him. He sees her out in the midst of a tidal wave, singing, beckoning to him, convinced as she is that she can save him with the power of their love. As he would gladly risk death rather than live his life without her, he dives into the wave as his shipmates go down with their vessel. She grabs a hold of him and carries him quickly down below to calmer waters where she thinks he'll be safe. His lungs collapse, and he dies instantly. She lives out the rest of her long life in sorrow and grief and shame, only understanding too late what she had done...

At a point, Dya noticed that Molly had stopped playing the guitar, but Dya kept her eyes closed, and continued to sing. The wind in the trees above was accompaniment enough.

When the song was complete, Dya opened her eyes to find her friends watching, spellbound, tears streaming down each of their cheeks.

Finally...

"Wow..." said Sarah, sniffling and wiping her face on the wolf blanket. "Wow."

And that is all that was said. They didn't ask a single question. They never even asked about the language. It truly did not matter, for the notes were universal.

She was happy to have been able to share this side of herself with them. It made her feel *honest*. More honest than she had been, even though they didn't understand the words.

However, Dya made a mental note to never mention this to

Mary Louise, certain as she was that it would upset her...for many reasons.

After a good while, watching the fire turn from licking flame to glowing red, Ethan suddenly sat up straight and said, "Oh man, I totally forgot!" He opened a yellow plastic cooler filled with thoroughly superfluous ice and began pulling out small, brown glass bottles. "Who wants a brewskinsky, eh?"

"I wish your pops would get a job at a new brewery," Malik said. "We need a change of flavor."

"Beggars can't be choosers, brother man," Ethan said, tossing a bottle to Malik who popped the cap off with his fingers. The two girls each took one as well. Dya's heart began pounding rapidly.

"Dy?" Ethan offered.

"Um," she stammered, "I don't...really...drink alcohol."

"Suit yourself," he said casually. "Let me know if you change your mind, eh. Damn, this one's not budging. Anybody got a lighter or a spoon or something I can break the seal with?"

"Here," Molly said, tossing Ethan a folded butterfly knife.

"Where'd you get this?"

"Take a guess."

"This Kendall's?"

"Not anymore, eh."

"Wicked." He edged the stubborn cap off easily with the tip of the knife.

Oh...to hell with it! Dya thought.

"I changed my mind," she said.

Ethan smiled and handed the freshly opened bottle over to her.

Here goes nothing, she thought.

She put the opening of the bottle up to her lips and allowed the cold liquid to pour into her mouth. It was bitter and sharp, and the hard little bubbles burned her tongue. She wanted to spit it out, but forced herself to swallow.

It's so awful! Why do they drink this?!

Suddenly, Dya felt herself getting light-headed. Her vision began to spread and warp, and a gray mist seemed to pass before her eyes. Her stomach wrenched, her face felt burned by an inner fire, and her mouth felt like sand. And then…it all went dark.

"Well, good morning, sleepyhead!"

Dya awoke the next morning inside the tent, bundled up tight in a sleeping bag and thick down quilt, her head pounding like a machine press.

"You know," Molly said to her, sipping from a mug of steaming hot coffee, "I'm pretty much of a lightweight myself. But you, girlie, are the grand champion high priestess of featherweights. Color me astonished, eh."

"What happened?" Dya groaned. Just speaking out loud made her temples throb.

"You had a sip of beer," Molly said. "A. Sip. As in one. One little sip of beer. And then you passed out. Sleep well did we?"

"Hmmmm…"

"Coffee?"

"No, thank you. Do we have tea?"

"Didn't think to bring any."

"Alas."

Dya considered for a brief moment that it would be a cheat to allow herself to heal from this. *That's not what normal people do on land!* After a few more painful seconds, however, she decided, *It's not like anyone will see.* She shut her eyes, and in a few short moments the hangover washed away, and she was as good as new. *No more of that, though. You're a land person now. Behave like one. No more of that. And no more beer either.*

"Pancakes!" Ethan announced. "Get 'em while they're black on the outside with a salmonella center!"

"So what are we doing today?" Dya asked as she accepted a

plate against her better judgment.

"We are gonna *conquer* this forest!" Malik replied, a triumphant fist in the air. "That's what we are going to do! Every stone inch!"

"Or," Sarah said, sipping her coffee, "we're just gonna wander around in the woods for a while, then head home cold and dirty."

"Yeah, whichever's good with me," Malik said with a shrug.

They spent the rest of the day hiking and taking pictures. As gorgeous as the landscape was, each photo ended up being just another excuse to mug about and fool around. They would pretend to be falling from cliffs, or act as if they were running from an axe murderer. Or were already butchered by the same and lay dead in the tangled weeds.

"Someday," Molly said, "when people ask me, Miss Jones, how did you spend your formative years? I will reply, 'Hacked to bits in a browning field.'"

"That would be a wicked song title, eh," Ethan said.

Dya couldn't help but notice a change in Malik, however. As the day went on, she saw him becoming more withdrawn and agitated. It was a subtle change, and no one else seemed to be aware. Dya said nothing, but more than once she saw him glancing desperately at his cell phone. There was no signal. Certainly he knew there would be no signal. But still he checked it, again and again.

"Goddamn phone sucks," he muttered. "Worthless piece of crap."

On the ride back into town, it was hard not to notice that Malik was growing distant and distracted. He drove, more or less in silence, the radio turned down very low. Much lower than usual. No one was quite sure what the matter was, not even Molly. But they opted not to press it.

***

Finally, as they rolled into Portland proper, Malik nervously said, "Guys...can I ask a huge, enormous favor of you all?"

"Of course, Mal," Sarah said, glad to have a break in the silence at last. "What's up, eh?"

"Um...my granddad...the one who gave me the tent...he's in...a home, all right? It's actually a bit...more than a nursing home. He's...well...he isn't long for the world, they think. And I haven't, you know, I haven't been to see him in a while. Um...because...it's just hard. You know what I'm saying? I mean; he's only sixty-nine years old. Hardly over retirement age. But the man is frail and withered...emphysema...He's barely able to speak, with all the breathing tubes and respirators he's hooked to and whatnot. Plus, he seems to be going through some early stages of dementia. Or at least...it was still in the early stages the last time I saw him."

"What happened to him?" Dya asked.

"Well, having ravaged his lungs and throat with cigarettes for fifty-plus years...it can take its toll, I'll say that much."

Dya felt a nervous sickness lurching up in the pit of her stomach.

"You want us to go with you, homie?" Molly asked, softly brushing Malik's dreads from his face. "Is that what it's all about? You know we will, eh. Right guys?"

Everyone else chimed in with affirmation:

"Of course we will." "Come on." "Let's go there now."

Though Dya was apprehensive, she did not voice it.

"Cool," Malik said, breathing a sigh of relief. "That is very cool." He turned the music up. And off they went.

The facility was warm and comforting. Deep earth tones coated the walls, and soft music lilted through the overhead speakers. The lady at the front desk smiled to Malik in recognition when they walked in, and waved them through without a word.

"Let me go in first," Malik said. "He might not be awake. Or he might be super medicated."

"You sure, babe?" Molly asked.

"Yeah, I don't want to overwhelm him right away."

Sarah, Ethan, Dya, and Molly waited out in the carpeted hallway as Malik entered the room alone.

"Granddad?" they heard him say softly. "Hey granddad. It's me. Malik. How you doing?" They heard a muffled murmur of faint recognition. "You're looking good. It's great to see you. They treating you okay in here?" The same mumble of vague affirmation was heard. "I've brought some friends with me. We just went camping and we used your old army tent. Yeah! Yeah, it worked real good! We didn't get attacked by Viet Cong or anything, ha ha. Would you like to meet them? Molly's here. You remember me telling you about her? The girl from the old complex? Yep, that's her. She's the one. Yeah, she's here, and she'd sure like to meet you."

At this Molly's eyes welled with tears. She wiped them on her sleeve, cleared her throat and walked on in.

"Hi there, granddad!" the rest heard her say. "So wicked to meet you finally."

"You guys can come in too!" Malik shouted.

Ethan, Sarah, and Dya entered the small room to find Malik's grandfather, scrawny and withered, laying on his back, beeping monitors all around him, his thin face strapped to a clear plastic mask. Molly was holding his hand, and he squeezed back affectionately.

They could see him smile through the mask, his kind eyes not but dim slits.

At the sight of the man, though, Dya felt the knot that had been forming in the pit of her stomach twist harden, and the desire to flee before he got a good look at her burned hot.

***

Marvin...Oh god, Marvin...

It was too late.

Upon seeing her, the old man's eyes shot wide open in shock. In an instant he flew into thrashing hysterics, groaning out in a vain attempt to scream, unable to articulate at all.

"NAAAAAAAAAAAAAAAAAAAAHHHH!!!"

"Granddad?!" Malik shouted in alarm. "What is it?! Granddad! *Nurse!!!*"

Three nurses instantly rushed in.

"Cain't be!" the old man screamed through the mask. "*Cain't be!*"

"Mr. Myers! Sir! Please calm down!"

The old man continued to thrash about, moaning in unintelligible horror. No one but Dya realized that he was looking directly at her. They all thought he was simply having "an episode."

But she knew better.

And she felt helpless.

And she felt like running away.

The nurses quickly administered a sedative, and Marvin Myers drifted fitfully off to sleep.

Malik appeared shaken, but not terribly surprised.

"I'm sorry you guys had to see that," he said quietly.

"It's okay, baby," Molly said, sniffling, holding tight and kissing him, tears dripping down her face. "We're just glad to be here with you. Aren't we, guys."

"Absolutely, bro," Ethan said. "Hey, it's all right. Old man's tough, eh. He'll wake up in a few hours, and he'll have totally forgotten about the whole thing. Come back tomorrow and you'll see. Everything'll be wicked good then."

"He doesn't forget anything," Malik whispered. "He never forgets."

Marvin, Dya said inside her head, *please be okay...please...be okay...*

Serious Complications

There was another difficulty as well. A far more serious one to be sure. Over time, I was beginning to find that transforming, either for the sea or for solid ground, was becoming more and more painful, and more difficult. As time went on, it became excruciating. I would grow dizzy and nauseous merely from the attempt.

I thought perhaps that it was because I was trying to change too close to land. Maybe the water was too warm and thin there. This seemed especially plausible when Mary Louise and her family moved to Ogunquit and its warmer climate. So I would be sure to dive further down beforehand, making my full transformation much deeper below the surface. That turned out to be unwise. At least once I nearly drowned doing so.

I could not figure out what I was doing wrong. But ever more, I was getting sicker and sicker. Sometimes my lungs would not properly expand or contract right away; less of a problem crawling up to the shore from the sea, but potentially deadly if I was trying to return to the deep. Or, patches of my legs would remain silver for longer and longer stretches of time after coming ashore.

I found myself needing a lengthier recovery time upon my return. I was terrified. I didn't know what was the matter with me, and there was no one for me to speak with about it. I was on my own.

Regardless, I was determined to keep this new sickness from Mary Louise. I did not want her to worry, though she was far too perceptive to hide it from her forever.

"Dya, are you okay? You don't look well."

"I'm fine."

"You're clearly not. What's the matter?"

"I'm just fine. Really."

We had begun discussing the possibility of me staying...for good. A terrifying prospect, let there be no doubt, to leave my family and my life as I had known it behind. Nothing was concrete just yet, just a "what if." But it was starting to become starkly clear to me that I could not keep splitting my time between the two worlds. It was, quite literally, tearing me apart.

My fateful decision was clinched the week of Mary Louise's sixteenth birthday (which we decided was my sixteenth birthday as well). I had taken to coming ashore only in the dead of night, partially to avoid being spotted, but also because it often afforded me at least a couple of minutes to vomit out my rapidly worsening transformation sickness and make the full change before Mary Louise would find me and supply me with an outfit to wear.

After a particularly rough change, and having finally pulled myself together, I wobbled out on unsteady feet from behind my rocky cover to be greeted by—

"Well hellooooo, love!"

There Mary Louise stood on the soft white sandy beach in an affected pose, barefoot but otherwise looking very much like Audrey Hepburn in a slim skirt and pill-box hat. She held a lit cigarette in her fingers, though I did not see her actually smoke it.

"Well aren't we all dolled up," I whispered, shivering and dripping.

"A bit of an early birthday present, daaahling," she said handing over a towel and my clothes. They were, like hers, brand new, and rather too upscale to be yanked over a cold, naked, salt-water soaked body at midnight. "Happy birthday to us both."

"Happy birthday," I whispered, toweling off quickly and sliding awkwardly into the clothes.

"Don't worry, I have PJs for you at the house," she said, dropping the 'glamour girl' shtick. "I just wanted to see how the new duds fit. They look simply smashing on you."

"They're great, thanks."

"Don't mention it, love. We'll have to wear them out on the town sometime soon. I told Mom you were coming and would be staying with us for the week. She's fine with it. Oh, if she asks, Francine and Bill are on a second honeymoon in Tuscany."

"Who?"

"Your parents, *remember?*"

"Oh. Yes. Bill and Francine." Pause. "Tuscany?"

"Sounded romantic."

"My parents might actually be in Tuscany for all I know."

We began to walk back up to her house. I would periodically stumble, still on shaky legs, and she would simply grab me around my waist for support.

"Easy now, hon," she said, helping me back up straight. She had taken to calling me 'hon,' 'love,' and 'sweetheart' the previous summer, initially as a joke. But before long, they had stuck.

"I'm okay," I said, allowing my voice to step up a touch above the whisper.

"So anyway," she said in what was a poor attempt at a casual tone, "I have news."

"Yes?"

"I mean, it's not really a big deal or anything."

"Tell me."

"Oh, it's just that I have…a boyfriend."

"You do?" The pitch of my voice was louder than I had

wanted, but this genuinely took me by surprise.

She squealed and did a happy little dance.

"His name is Marvin. He's already seventeen. His family is considering moving up here from way down south somewhere. And, he is...an absolute dream. Oh, and he looks, just a little tiny bit, like a younger Elmore James. Something about the shape of his chin."

"I can't wait to meet him."

"You're just going to love him, Dya. But hands off, sister, he's all mine!"

We laughed, although I knew she was only somewhat kidding. Romantic jealousy, I was aware even then, is a very powerful impulse in this culture. As is its corresponding possessiveness. Wars on land have been fought over less. It made little sense to me, for such an issue is nonexistent in the deep. It still seems enormously silly and pointless to me.

I stopped her before we stepped up to the porch.

"Mary Louise, I have news too."

"What is it, dahling?" she replied, once again affecting the high-society pose and daintily holding the cigarette close to her lips without actually touching.

"I'm staying."

The unsmoked cigarette fell from her fingers.

"What?"

"I'm staying."

"You...you are?"

"I've decided. My mind is made up. I want to be here. From now on. As in forever."

"Are...you serious, Dya?"

"Deadly."

"You...you promise?"

"I promise. More and more, I'm just not happy in the deep. I'm only happy here. This is where I feel like I belong. I miss the land when I'm gone, and I miss you. I don't want to go back home. I want to make my home up here. I've been wondering why, over the past couple of years, we've been getting *older side by side, you and me. And I've decided that it's fate, I think. If I had stayed in the deep I'd still just be a nine- or ten-year-old girl, for all intents and purposes. Well to hell with that I say!"*

For a frozen moment Mary Louise simply stared at me, her mouth open in shock. Then, from out of nowhere, she screamed and threw her arms around me. I returned the embrace and we both laughed and cried.

"This is going to be sooooo great!" she exclaimed. "We are going to have a blast*!*" I was deliriously happy too…"We'll go to college together!" she said. "We'll share an apartment in the city!"…and I was also scared beyond my wits. "It'll just be the most, Dya! You'll see!"

The Best Kept Secret in Town

Malik's granddad died in late November. On a Wednesday. His funeral was the following Friday. For the occasion Mary Louise bought Dya her first black dress in over fifty years. She wished that she would never have to wear it again. Sadly, she would.

The "episode" Marvin Myers experienced never repeated. Never so much as mentioned again. Prior to his passing Malik even seemed to think that his grandfather was improving. Somewhat. Then, one morning, the nurses found him not breathing. He had drifted off in his sleep, never to wake again.

"I'm happy," Malik said. "I am really happy for him to have gone the way he did."

"You don't look happy," said Dya.

"But I am."

Dya had never been inside a church before. And she could not say that she much cared for it. In fact, she hated it. She could not fathom how people found solace in such a horrible place. At the wake, Mary Louise spent a good amount of time with Malik. Giving comfort and wisdom. No one knew what she said to him, but it seemed to help. He nodded a lot at what she said, dabbing his wet eyes against the sleeves of his black suit. Dya wondered how much she was sharing with him. She also couldn't help but notice how nice he looked in his suit. Not that it mattered.

For her part, once she looked, Dya could not pull her eyes away from the casket. And she could not stop crying, though she did not want to make a show of it. For all anyone but Mary Louise knew, Marvin Myers had simply been the grandfather of one of her best friends. Nothing more. They did not need to know different.

Marvin...dearest Marvin...you were such a sweet and handsome boy...

"Granddad bought me my first drum kit," Malik said, vowing not to let the grief get the better of him. "I owe it to him to make the most of my music. It's time to get this band going, you guys. Let's make it happen. Who's with me?"

"You know we are, eh," said Ethan.

Confirmation all around.

They set up a rehearsal space in Sarah's mother's garage and rocked out on covers. Badly at first, mostly just making a noisy mess of Baroness and Kylesa songs, with the occasional old Crisis cut thrown in for good measure.

"This stuff's hard, eh," Ethan said. "Is it too late to just be a punk rock band?"

"Yes it is," Molly answered.

Over time, however, they improved. Molly taught them her original songs, which were far more advanced than one might expect from a musician her age. She and Malik locked in perfectly together, and Ethan did his best to keep up and serve as a bridge between them, his skills sharpening by the day.

Everyone prodded Dya to "let loose" with her voice, which of course, she did not do. Instead she simply practiced at making it sound *as if* she were screaming at the top of her lungs, careful always to switch off the microphone.

They're my friends, after all. I really don't want, if at all possible, to make their skulls explode all over the garage.

"You know what," Malik said after a particularly rocking practice, "damn it all if we ain't getting pretty damn tight up in here."

"Are we maybe possibly ready to play a show? Maybe?" Molly asked, although clearly she already had her answer.

"I'm down if you guys are, eh," said Ethan blowing on his sore fretting fingers. Molly's songs were nothing if not a workout.

"We need a name though, right?" Dya asked.

"How about we call ourselves Dya-bolical," Ethan said.

Laughter all around.

"Can I just go ahead and ixnay that one?" Dya said.

"Seconded," Molly replied.

"Duh, you guys," said Sarah. "There's only one name that could ever be for this band." The other four all looked at her quizzically. "It's so obvious, eh!" They leaned in toward her expectantly. "*Leviathan!*"

"Sare," Malik said, "I'm pretty sure there is another band called Leviathan already. I'd put money on it."

"There is," Ethan said. "I've heard 'em."

"So then let them sue us," Sarah replied with a shrug. "Think of the publicity, eh. And then we'll just change it to Leviathan ME."

"But won't people assume we're a Mastodon cover band or something?" Dya asked.

"And that would be bad why exactly?" Sarah answered.

No one could argue with her logic.

Upon further exploration they discovered that indeed *Leviathan* was already the name of *several* bands. As was *Leviathan Rising*. And also *The Leviathans*. Even *We Are The Leviathans*.

"*We Are The Leviathans?!* What the hell does that even mean, eh?"

"No need to be salty just because they got to it first."

"On the contrary, that is a perfectly good reason to be salty."

So, after much discussion, they decided upon *Leviathan Immortal*.

"All right," Molly said, "now instead of simply ripping off another band, we're ripping off *two*! That's a good plan."

Over the Moon

She was right about Marvin. Funny and charming...and so very handsome. And the perfect gentleman, which he credited to his, "South'rn raisin'," which made Mary Louise giggle uncontrollably (though I don't truly understand why).

It had been Marvin who gave Mary Louise her first cigarette, a habit she grew quickly tired of after a couple of days (sadly, Marvin did not). The three of us had a marvelous time that week, and it made me glad to see Mary Louise so over-the-moon happy. The first time I saw the two of them kiss, I thought it looked nice and that maybe I'd like to do that too. Not with Marvin necessarily, but with someone.

We hit it off well right from the start, Marvin and I, just as Mary Louise hoped we would. Had I known better of such things, I suppose I should have felt like what they call a "third wheel." But I didn't. I liked him, I loved her, they were sweet on each other...what's the harm? And besides, I never understood that metaphor anyway. Depending upon the vehicle, third wheels can be quite useful, after all.

Marvin had brought with him quite a collection of records. Music from down south we had never heard before. Music that completely blew our hair black. Music that made even Mr. Elmore James (whom Marvin did indeed resemble, if only ever so slightly) sound quiet and subdued by comparison. I loved it. I loved every last bit of it.

THE SONG IN THE SQUALL

"You need to hear Dya sing sometime," Mary Louise said to Marvin as the two of them danced close. "Her voice is so glorious."

"Well lay sumthin' on me, little lady!"

"It doesn't sound like this stuff, that's for sure," I said, swinging my hips in rhythm to some sweat-breaking barrelhouse beat.

"That's ai'ight. Let's hear it!"

"Maybe later."

Maybe later...maybe...

"You promise?"

"Well..."

"Pretty please cherries and all?"

"I'll do my best."

It was a promise I had not intended to keep.

Something in the Way

She knew it was a mistake. She knew she shouldn't do it. But sitting in the library during her morning free period, Dya couldn't help but look up the website. The website people snickered about as she walked by in the hallway. The one Trina Beckett and her girl friends had set up.

"Freak Alert!" it was called. Dya was not the only freak on the site, of course, and indeed her four friends were there as well (though there wasn't much about them other than the fact that they were a bunch of filthy, homeless dope addicts).

But there, at the top of the page was the spotlighted *Freak of the Week*, and a photo of Dya, teary and terrified in the girls' bathroom, accompanied by a graphic description of all the things she would be willing to do, and for very little money to boot.

Dya's face burned hot, and she felt sick to her stomach—not so much because of all the supposedly "sluttish" activities she was game for (about which, admittedly, she was largely indifferent), but because of the open comments section below. Beyond the standard "LULZ" and ":P" and "OMG what a trash-dump skank!"-type fare, some people had posted:

"Ugly, stoopid, foreign, whutz new? Go back 2 where u cum from u pig."

"A Ryme 4 DIE-a when she comz herre: ONE FISH TWO FISH DEAD BITCH YOU BITCH"

"I wish this #%&ing %$&* wud do the wrld a favr and just

THE SONG IN THE SQUALL

#$%^ing K-LL HERSLF!"

And on and on.

Dya calmly X'ed out of the site, stood up from her chair, and slowly walked out of the library. Her eyes blurry. A twisting knot in her throat she could not swallow away.

At least I know what they really think of me. At least now I know for sure.

There, alone behind the old equipment shed, right where she had last seen Jimmie Kendall, Dya sat in the un-mowed grass, her knees under her chin. She shut her eyes tight as hot tears dripped from her cheeks onto her jeans.

She sang softly to herself, an ancient song. But, soothing as it may have sounded, it was no lullaby. It was a song for *murder*, meant specifically to lure a wayward boatswain to his death. Beautiful and seductive if one did not comprehend the subtext. And its victims never did. Dya had never understood why she had been taught these songs as a young girl, for her people no longer practiced this barbaric and malicious act.

But I understand it now, she thought. *Now I understand for damn sure.*

Her anger was at war with her sadness and her shame. Thankfully she was alone, and there was no one about to hear the song.

So she thought.

Hearing footsteps in the grass, Dya quickly shut her mouth mid-phrase and opened her eyes. Standing but a few yards from her, sweaty and red and lightly panting from his morning laps, was Brad Pitre. Steam rose from him in the damp, chilly air. They watched one another in silence for a moment or two, then Brad

jogged off, still with a look of stunned confusion across his face.
*Damn it...*Dya thought...*I should never come here.*

"So," Ethan said as they all convened at their usual spot in the lunchroom, "we've hit another snag, eh."

"What's up?" Malik asked, munching half-heartedly on a bag of cool-ranch Doritos. "Not that I'm surprised. I'd be more shocked if all was smooth sailing."

Dya laughed quietly, keeping her hair down in an attempt to mask any lingering signs of crying that remained on her face. She simply did not feel like having to explain it to her friends. Certainly there were more pressing matters at hand.

"Well anyway," Ethan continued, "I've been calling around. All-age venues are in wicked short supply in these parts. So, booking a show somewhere established that might have a built-in audience is looking to be something of what one might charitably call a no-go."

"We just need to get an opening slot on a bill with a bigger band," Molly said, nursing a generic orange soda. Her father had packed her a tuna fish sandwich she opted not to eat.

"Therein lies the rub, Moll," Ethan. "We don't know anybody who'll let us open. We don't know anybody at all. I don't even know if there *is* a scene in Portland, eh."

"What about those bands we went to see in October?" Dya suggested.

"Tried 'em," Ethan said. "They weren't having it. Guess I can't blame them. Who wants a buncha high schoolers dragging down the bill."

"So what should we do?" Dya asked. "I mean, I've never played a show before, so I don't know the protocol."

"Except for Sarah, who did a tap dance for her third grade talent show," Malik said, "*none* of us have ever played a show before."

"It wasn't tap dancing, eh," Sarah said, "it was *clog* dancing."

"I sit corrected."

"Why is Brad Whatsisname staring at us?" Molly asked.

Dya looked up across the lunchroom, and Brad quickly turned his eyes away from her and back to whatever his A-Crowd chums were jabbering on about.

"Well," Ethan said with a sigh, still focused on the situation at hand, "okay...hear me out on this. A friend of my pops works maintenance at a downtown office complex, eh. And he has keys to an old, empty storefront. Don't know who owns it, but it's been vacant since forever. I think the place used to sell washing machines or something. There's probably still some there rusting in the corners. But anyway...I called him up yesterday and kinda tried to smooth talk him."

"Bet that went well," Malik said, deadpan.

"Smooth talk him into what exactly?" Molly asked.

"Dig it," Ethan said, his hands up as if to say *Keep an open mind*, "I think I've maybe got him convinced to let us use the space, eh, as long as we can return it to the exact condition it's currently in."

"You suggesting we put together our own show top to bottom, baby?" Sarah asked. "No actual venue, no other bands, just, *Ladies and Gentlemen we give you Leviathan Immortal?*"

"I know," Ethan grumbled, prematurely defeated. "It's totally crazy, eh. Who would come, right? Nobody, that's who. Not even our parents."

"My mom would come if booze was provided," said Sarah.

"Your mom's a drunken whore. No offense."

"I don't know E," Molly said with a thoughtful expression and that devious twinkle in her eye. "I think the idea might just have merit."

"Y—You do? Really?"

"Why not, eh?"

"But...we'll just be playing to a room full of washing machines!"

"At least they won't boo us," said Dya.

"I wouldn't count on that."

"I definitely think it warrants further exploration," Malik said.

Ethan sat silently, gobsmacked that his friends warmed to the idea so quickly, when he was barely committed to it himself.

"Let's try to put the feelers out in our classes today and tomorrow," Molly said. "Try to gauge if we think folks might come out over winter break to bang their heads and get their wild on."

"It couldn't hurt," Dya said, although she knew full well that she would not be asking anyone in any of her classes if they would come to her performance. She did not speak in class. Ever. As much as she wanted to play a good show, she simply did not have the gumption to say a word of this out loud to people who by all counts hated her reflexively.

Hopefully everyone else is braver than I am...

"Oh, it could always hurt, Dy," Ethan said. "It could *always* hurt."

They all bade each other "see ya," and headed off in different directions, with a tentative commitment to explore the solo show further. Malik walked Dya to her *Ancient and Medieval History* class, which was right across the hall from his *Geometry II*. They didn't speak much along the way, but as they neared their respective classrooms, Malik said, "So, did ya see the site?"

"What site?" Dya asked, trying to play dumb.

"Come on, Dy, I'm on there too, you know."

"Oh. Yeah."

Dya felt her lip begin to tremble, but she sucked it up and shook it off, determined to not let it get to her.

"Hey," Malik said, sensing how upset she was, "Hell with those people, all right?" Dya nodded, watching her sandaled feet scuff along across the tiled floor.

"It's not a big deal," she whispered, because that was all she could get her voice to do.

THE SONG IN THE SQUALL

Malik stopped walking. Dya did as well.

"Dya, look at me."

She looked up into his eyes right there in the middle of hallway.

"Hey, move your asses, eh!" Somebody shouted at them. Not wanting to get into a row just then, Malik took Dya's hand and led her to the left-side lockers.

"Seriously," Malik said, his kind eyes and warm smile lighting up his soft, smooth face. "Who gives a crap what a bunch of dumb jack-offs think anyhow. *We* love you. And, unlike the aforementioned jack-offs, *we* actually matter." Dya giggled and looked off, blushing just a shade. "And we know none of that junk on there is true."

"What if it were true?"

"Hey, whatever," Malik replied, smiling all the wider. "Cool with me. I'm just glad my lead singer made *Freak of the Week*. You can't buy that that kind of publicity!"

They both laughed out loud. Dya had not noticed that they were still holding hands until Malik gave hers a little squeeze.

"Chin up, homie," he said.

"I'm fine. Really."

"You sure?"

"Totally."

"I'll see ya later."

"'Kay," Dya replied, barely above a whisper once again. As she watched him limp off to class she felt the knot return to her throat, though it was nowhere near as painful as it had been.

Careless Girl

Late Wednesday evening, Mary Louise had one of her migraines. And it was a doozy. She lay in her bed, drawn up tight as a drum with her arms and legs wrapped around a pillow, her eyelids squeezed shut from the pain. I rubbed her temples with my fingertips.

"Is that helping at all?"

"A little," she said in a pinched whisper.

"I hate when you feel this way."

"Dya..."

"What can I do for you?"

But, of course, I knew what she was going to ask for.

"Just a little song. Okay? Just a short one."

"Mary Louise...I really—"

"Please?"

"They're dangerous. I really shouldn't."

"I know. But...just this once. And I won't ask ever again. Or...I won't ask for a very long while. Promise."

So, I relented. As I nearly always did. And as I sang, her tension eased. I saw her arms and legs and eyelids loosen their grip. Tears dripped from her eyes onto her pillow, carrying at least a bit of the pain with them.

Drain away...drain all away...

As softly as I could, I eased myself out of the bed, and crept lightly across the hard wood floor.

THE SONG IN THE SQUALL

"Could you close the window?" she asked, already drifting. "Even the ocean is too loud tonight."

I did, and she was asleep before the bedroom door was shut behind me.

I stepped outside into the cool evening. The salty sea mist on the breeze was delicious, and tantalizing, and I breathed it in deeply.

It occurred to me just then that, if I were truly staying on land, then that would mean I would never so much as see the deep again. It seemed so obvious in that moment, and yet I truly had not given it the complete consideration it warranted. Did that mean that I would never swim again? At all? Ever? The thought filled me with a sudden, hollow despair. I had not fully grasped the larger ramifications of it all.

Out sitting just in from the lap of the tide, I saw a figure. Walking closer, I could see that it was Marvin, smoking what was hopefully his last cigarette for the night.

"Hi, Marvin."

"Whatcha say there, Dya," he answered. But, oddly, he would not look up at me. Instead he stared out into the black waves, and the starlight that danced across their surface.

"Out for a late night walk?"

"Mah folks is fightin'," he replied. "Needed a breather from the tension, hear? Was gonna stop by to see if Mary Louise was feelin' any better. Her headaches is a monster f'sho."

"I know," I said, sitting down beside him. He still did not look over at me. I dug my bare toes into the sugar-white sand. His tennis shoes and striped socks were caked with wet sand, as if he had been wading out into the surf.

That's not safe for you to do, I thought. But I said nothing.

We sat in silence for a while, until he finally said, his voice nearly a-tremble,

"What...what was that song?"

Oh no!

He must have been walking past the open window while I was singing.

"It's just...just an old f-folk song," I stammered in reply. "That's all."

"I ain't never heard no language like that befo'," he said, talking a deep drag from his cigarette. He ashed it in the sand before carefully balling up the remainder and placing it in the pocket of his shirt. "I ain't never heard no melody like 'at. And I know music pretty darn well."

"Well...there's a whole big world out there."

"I reckon."

"Are you...okay?"

"So...nev' mind."

"What?"

"So...where...where you come from, huh?"

"From away."

"I ain't no Mainer, Dya. That mess don't play with me."

He looked over at me, and our eyes locked. The look in his eyes was that of sheer terror...and pure longing. But not for me. I knew that. It was for the song. And, although there was no earthly way he could have possibly known what I was, I got the strong sense that he knew I was...different. That I wasn't just odd. I was "other." I felt like I should get away, quickly, before there was any more regret to go around.

"Don't go jus' yet."

"Okay..."

"Your eyes..."

"What about them?"

"They...ain't hazel...in this light..."

I thought I should turn away. But I didn't.

"It's just the moon. It plays tricks."

"What secrets you got, girl?" he whispered.

"I...I..."

"Can you tell me?"

"I...I can't...I don't..."

"*You can. Tell me.*"

"*No...I...*"

We stared into each other's eyes for a painfully long time.

"You ain't got to say, if you don't want," he said finally, turning away from me. "I don't blame you if'n you cain't. But...I..." He swallowed hard. "I sure...would like to hear that song again."

"It was a mistake," I said. "I'm sorry. You shouldn't have heard." And it was foolish of me to have sung it. There were other songs, after all. Different songs I could have sung. Less powerful songs. Less enticing. On occasion, my uncles are right about me. I can sometimes be a very stupid, careless girl.

Marvin nodded, and exhaled deeply, and looked off again toward the rippling sea. I stood up to head back inside.

"I need to go. Mary Louise might be looking for me."

"I s'spect she might," he said, distant.

"Good night, Marvin. I'll see you tomorrow, okay?"

"Good night, m'lady," he said. "Whoever you are."

We planned to have a little birthday party for Mary Louise (and me) on Saturday, just her parents and the three of us. Although nothing was ever said about it, and I cannot say for sure exactly why, over the next couple of days Mary Louise seemed particularly clingy to Marvin whenever he was around. As if she did not want he and I to ever be alone together. Which, although not entirely necessary, was not perhaps altogether unwise.

Did she suspect that something had happened between Marvin and me? Should I tell her that nothing had? How serious was their relationship anyway? Might I need to ultimately share The Big Secret with him? If so, when? How would I share it? What would he say? What would he do? In the short time that I knew him, Marvin struck me as tremendously wise and perceptive for his young age. Far more so than Mary Louise's parents, who should have had way more questions for—and about—me than they did. I don't know. I have always been a curious girl—too *curious—and I can usually spot a fellow traveler when I meet one. Not always...but often.*

As it was, it was clear enough (at least to me), that Marvin did not want to be alone with me anyway, for any reason. Though he was never rude or obvious, I nonetheless cannot remember him ever looking me in the eyes again.

And those truly were just my hazel eyes.

A Slip and a Twist

"Weenies!" Molly shouted, calf-deep in the frigid water. "Weenies all!"

Her friends rightly ignored her, as only a deranged fool would wade into the ocean off the coast of Maine in December. Sarah sat on the rocks, sketching and storyboarding her on-stage video projections the old-fashioned way: pencils and drafting paper. And lots of erasing. Malik and Ethan pitifully attempted to toss a football back and forth, which frequently landed in the water, forcing Molly to retrieve it for them. The fierce wind stabbed and slashed at their skin, but this was where they all wanted to be.

"So what's the plan exactly, eh?" Ethan asked, missing yet another pass.

"The plan is what the plan is," Malik replied. "We set up the gear, hope an audience shows up, and then we proceed to rock their theoretical faces off. That's it."

"We've definitely got the venue," Ethan replied. "It's the audience that still concerns me."

"It's simple," Molly shouted from the water, freezing cold but not admitting it. "Middle of the winter, nothing to do, all-ages venues in short supply, we message-blast every single high schooler in the greater Portland area, and folks will be so desperate for some fun they'll settle for us."

"But nobody likes us, eh!" Ethan. "I mean nobody likes us *personally*. I casually tried to invite folks from every single one of my classes and was answered with an icy blast of silent hostility. And those were the *good* replies."

The rest concurred. They had gotten a roughly similar response. Similarly rough.

"Okay," Sarah interjected, "but kids at the *other* schools don't know that, eh. They haven't had the opportunity to preemptively dislike us."

"Yeah, that'll happen in due time," said Malik tripping and fumbling the ball.

Ethan sighed and shook his head. "I love this plan, eh. I'm thrilled to be a part of it."

"Hey," said Molly, "we gotta try at least."

"Dya!" Ethan shouted up the rocks. "You got something to add to this discussion? You are the lead singer after all!"

Dya had gone exploring up the rocks. They hadn't seen her in quite a while, but assumed that she wasn't too far off.

"*What*?!" came a faint shout from some distance.

"*Do! You! As! Front-person! Have! Any! Opin—*"

But he was cut off by a horrible cracking sound and the echoing blast of a blood-curdling scream.

"*Dya!?*" Molly called out, climbing quickly out of the water and up the cold stones. "Dya, are you okay?!" The rest-followed suit, scampering as fast as they could up the rocky shore side.

Another sickening crack and Dya's shriek once again pierced the air.

"Oh god!" Malik said. "Dya, where are you?!"

At the top of the small cliff, they saw Dya's figure off a short ways in silhouette with the sun directly behind her. Doubled over, only her left leg was visible.

"I'm stuck!" Dya screamed in agony as her friends ran toward her as best they could along the cold, uneven jags. "My feet slipped! I can't get my right foot out!"

Sure enough, there they found her, her foot wedged deep into a cluster of sharp, jagged rocks. Around her leg and across the rocks fresh blood glistened in the sunlight.

"Ohhhh, this is not good," Molly said, trying to control the warbling panic in her voice. She got down on her knees for a closer look. "Dya, don't struggle, you're going to break your toes."

"I think...I've already...broken my toes," Dya said, her teeth tight together, tears streaming down her lightly freckled cheeks.

Damn...I should not have said that...Now I'm committed...

"Well, let's try to not make it worse, eh," Molly said. "Malik, give me your shirt. Once we get her foot out we need to wrap it, cuz it's bleeding wicked bad."

Malik pulled his green, checkered flannel over his head and handed it to Molly, trying not to shiver in just a long-john top. He, Ethan and Sarah helped Dya down slowly into a sitting position to take the pressure off, ready to pick her up once she was free of the rocks.

"Okay, girl," Molly said to Dya in the calmest voice she could muster, "we're gonna slide your foot out, okay? We'll do it slow, but it's gonna tickle a bit coming out. Ready?"

Dya nodded, sweat beading and freezing on her face. They tried to pull her gently back to ease the process. No luck. They tried again and again. Nothing. And again. It would not budge. It took all of Dya's strength not to shatter the sky with a scream of pain at the slightest twist of her ankle.

"Should we call an ambulance or something?" Sarah said. "Or, like, the fire department maybe? What's the proper procedure here?"

"Guys," Dya said through further clenched teeth, "Let's just...do it quickly."

"I really don't think that's a good idea, eh," Sarah said, her voice quivering at the sight of the blood spattered heavily around the rocks.

"We have to, or I'll be stuck here forever. Please. Let's just...I can handle it."

I can handle it...I can handle it...

They all looked to Molly. For whatever reason, Molly always

seemed to have final say on such matters.

Finally, Molly simply threw up her hands and said, "If you say so, dude. I just, um, hope...oh god...oh god...okay...never mind. Okay."

They counted down, three...two...one...*pull!* As Dya's bare, bloody foot came free of the stone, a horrid snapping sound was heard. Dya buried her face in Ethan's chest, wailing, and muffled though it was, the power of the scream vibrated through Ethan's entire body like a shock wave. His eyes bulged open from the vibration, but he held tightly to her.

Bleeding profusely and nauseous with agony, Dya held up her twisted, gashed, rapidly purpling foot to Molly so she could wrap it in the flannel shirt.

"This really is not good at all," Molly said again, hands shaking. "Really, really so not good."

"I'll be fine," Dya wheezed with a hard shiver.

"Maybe someday, girlfriend," Molly said with a thin smile. "But not anytime soon you won't."

"We're gonna try to stand you up," Malik said to Dya, "Keep all your pressure on your left leg."

"Not yet, Mal," Molly said working the flannel tourniquet, "She's got a nasty gash we need to tie off here. Somewhere..."

Dya shut her eyes tightly and concentrated. *Stay hurt...you must stay hurt...*

She struggled to focus her attention on the pain. *Keep it. Maintain it. Do not...*

Do not heal...do...not...heal...It must hurt...it needs to hurt...

However, as Molly softly dabbed the blood from Dya's foot with the corner of the green flannel, she found herself doubting her very own eyes. Although it certainly could not be, simply could not be possible, there appeared to no longer be a source for all the blood. No cut, no gash, no wound whatever. Just a bit of dark blue bruising.

Molly looked up at Dya, unable to read the terrified, pleading look in her eyes.

"Dy," Molly said softly, "you can't...you can't wiggle your toes, can you?"

"No freaking way, dude!" Ethan said, hooking Dya's right arm over his shoulder. "She shouldn't even try, eh!"

"Can you?" Molly asked again.

She looked down, and suddenly Dya's thin, perfect toes flexed slowly back and forth, as if they'd never broken. Not so much as a nick or a bruise to be seen.

"Not as bad as I thought," said Dya, smiling weakly.

Shocked, Molly said nothing, but simply finished wrapping the miraculously uninjured foot. Sarah, Ethan, and Malik, oblivious to what Molly had just seen (or not seen) and not knowing that Dya no longer required assistance, helped her to stand. She pretended to need them and leaned heavily on their shoulders, periodically whimpering...as if in pain.

"So which hospital?" Malik asked as they trundled on over the rocks and back to the car.

"No hospital," said Dya quickly. "No, I need to see Marie Louise. I'm...on her insurance. If she thinks I need to go, she'll take me."

"She can meet us there, eh," Ethan said. "Let's not be risky with this. I'll call her right now."

"No, I really...just want to go home first."

"That's crazy."

"That's what I want to do."

"Okay," Malik said, "to grandmother's house we go then."

"Guess we should forget about the show for a while," Sarah said as they walked on toward the car. "We can call it off. No biggie, eh. 'Til Spring or whatever."

"No," Dya said. "Don't say that. I'll do it. I can do the performance. I'll be fine."

"Come on, guys," Molly said, trailing slightly behind the rest. "Dya's not gonna let a little thing like broken feet stop her from rocking out, eh?"

"Absolutely right," Dya said, looking back at Molly over Malik's shoulder, that same cryptic, pleading look in her eyes. "The show must go on."

For the next several days, Dya stayed home from school in order to perpetuate the ruse that she had significantly injured herself on the rocks. Mary Louise recommended, in the interest of consistency, that Dya try to limp or hop on one foot even when they were alone in the apartment. Dya tried her best, but it felt ludicrous, and often only did so when Mary Louise was looking.

One evening, as Dya lay on the living room couch reading, the ground floor doorbell chimed. Jumping up, she headed quickly over to the door before it rang again.

"Hello?" she said quietly into the intercom.

"*Hey, Dy. It's Malik. I've got your homework.*"

"I'll buzz you up."

She hit the unlock button for the downstairs door and immediately realized her mistake.

Oh, damn it!

She wasn't wearing the bandage around her foot, and in the time it would take to retrieve it from her bedroom and wrap her foot convincingly Malik would already be up the stairs. Indeed, in less than half a minute he knocked, and then walked in. She hobbled to the couch and eased herself into a sitting position, feigning a slight wince of pain in the process.

"How you feeling, girl?" Malik asked, dropping a handful of folders and a DVD on the counter of the kitchenette.

"It's still pretty sore," she said in a soft voice, "but nothing's broken. I'll be fine."

"Where's Mary Louise?"

"She had to lie down. She gets bad migraines sometimes. Has

since she was a little girl. Apparently."

"Ah, that sucks," Malik said, also lowering his voice. "Hope she's okay. Jesus, this is the house of pain up in here."

"Just needs time. All will be well. Thanks for bringing that stuff."

"No problem. Sarah gathered up most of it. I also dug out this old bootleg I transferred to DVD of the late, great Layne Staley playing with *Alice In Chains*. He's got a broken leg in the video, but he still manages to totally bring it live. I thought it might be, like, an inspiration or something."

"Thank you, I can't wait to watch it! I'm sure I'll be fine for the show, though. So Mal…" she said with a wry little grin, "I couldn't help but notice that you're wearing my blood."

Malik was in fact wearing the same green flannel shirt he wore the day of Dya's accident on the rocks.

He laughed. "Pretty metal, right? I tried to ZOUT it out, but it seems to have just locked it in further. Oh well, I don't have a lot of shirts, and it's one of my favorites, so why not. What's a little splattered blood between friends?" Dya giggled. "Now see, Dy, I would kinda assume, that instead of giggling at that, most girls would be a bit weirded out by it."

"Well, you do realize that I'm not like most girls, yes?"

They both laughed.

"True that, true that. So let me see how your war wound is doing."

She couldn't exact say no, as her bare foot was right there resting on the coffee table. With no small amount of reservation, she pulled up the cuff of her jeans to reveal a complete lack of injury. Her ankle, her toes, every bit of her foot was spotless and devoid of any visible damage.

"Damn, Wolverine!" Malik exclaimed, then covered his mouth sheepishly, worried that he might have disturbed Mary Louise. He continued in a much softer voice, "How the hell did you heal up so quickly?"

"I…I just don't bruise that much," Dya said, a nervous quiver in her voice betraying her ever so slightly. "But I think the tendon or ligament in my foot is torn maybe. It was swollen very badly last night, but it went down this morning. It still really hurts. A lot."

"Oh," said Malik, buying it, because he had no logical reason not to. "Still. Impressive, though."

Pause.

"Well...I think I'd better probably go check on Mary Louise."

"Yeah, I gotta roll out too. My sister needs her car back and all." He bent at the waist to assist her up. "Here, let me give you a hand."

As Malik helped her to her feet she leaned in to give him a customary hug goodbye. He returned the embrace and, although neither of them was sure who initiated it, they suddenly found themselves holding each other very close, their lips pressed against each other's. Dya felt a warmth spread across her face, and she shut her eyes.

The kiss froze them in time together for a moment or two; then reality returned as quickly as it had departed. Malik stepped awkwardly back (and Dya thought she heard a door click down the hallway. *Just my imagination...*)

"Damn," Malik said softly.

Yes...I'll say...

"That...that was..." he said. "Um...That was an accident. A mistake. I'm sorry. I'm really sorry."

It was? Yes...Yes it was...a mistake...

"I'm sorry," he said again.

"Don't be," she replied, softly, her head still swimming. "Don't be sorry. Things...just happen sometimes."

"Right. Right."

"It's not a big deal."

"I love Molly," Malik said out of the blue, fidgeting with his fingers awkwardly.

Could kissing me make you love her less somehow? Why

would that be?
"I love her too."
"I'd never want to hurt her."
"Never in a trillion years."
"Cool. Cool. So...uh...yeah. Our secret, right?"
"Absolutely."

They smiled at each other. It was a sad, embarrassed sort of smile. Although she did not fully understand why, Dya knew that, for whatever reason, something untoward had just happened.

It felt nice, though...

Malik headed over toward the door, the awkwardness of his gait appearing even more pronounced.

"I'll see ya tomorrow, Dya. I hope you dig the video. I think you will."

"I'm going to put it in tonight. Thanks again. I'll see you, Mal."

And with that Malik made his exit.

There inside the dark room, Dya found Mary Louise lying on her bed, facing the opposite wall. She appeared to be asleep, but Dya heard her quietly sniffling.

"Are you okay?" Dya asked softly. "Do you need anything? Some ice for your head maybe? Or just a cool rag?"

"It's getting a little better," Mary Louise answered with a light sniffle, "a couple of Ibuprofen might be good, though."

"Sure."

Dya retrieved two capsules from the medicine cabinet, sat on the bed, and handed them to Mary Louise who proceeded to swallow them dry without sitting up.

"Thanks, love."

"If you need anything let me know," Dya said, caressing her friend's head softly. "Try to get some sleep."

"I will. I'll be fine in the morning."

"Okay. I hope so."

Dya stood to leave.

"Dya?"

She stopped short at the door and turned her head.

"Yes?"

"Promise me…" Mary Louise sniffled. "Promise me, that you're not going to hurt those kids."

Dya's stomach squirmed, and she felt her face burning for the second time that evening, though in quite a different way. She felt hurt and ashamed, but clearly understood the request.

"Of course," she said. "Of course I won't. That's the last thing in the world that I want."

"I know it is. I know it is. Goodnight, sweetheart. I'll see you in the morning."

"Okay." Pause. "I love you."

"I love you too, hon."

Very Grown Up

The afternoon of "our" birthday party, I volunteered to go into town to pick up a few necessaries from the grocery for dinner. Mary Louise's father gave me some money, far more than what was likely needed, and I decided that I would use the rest to try and get Mary Louise a small present.

I seldom went to town alone, and it was oddly liberating to do so. A very grown-up feeling. I planned to stop in nearly every little shop along the strip, just to have a peak around. To look at me you'd never have any suspicion in the world that I didn't belong there (...or so I thought). However, although I always enjoyed the walk, I was not inclined to turn down a ride.

"Hey there, Dya. Goin' to town?""

By the side of the road I saw Marvin, sitting in the driver's seat of a sky-blue wagon with wood panels. He looked just a touch too young to be driving such a large vehicle. It was a funny sight, made all the sillier by his severe demeanor.

"Hey there yourself. And yes I am."

He turned the key, and the engine fired.

"Hop in."

"This your father's car?" I asked as we pulled out into traffic.

He nodded, his eyes dead set on the road ahead. Hands at two and ten, as they say.

"Pontiac Wood Grained Deluxe. Love of Old Man's life. Mama hates it, but she don't drive anyhow."

"Well, the heart only has so much room after all."

"Sho' nuff."

He was driving particularly slow.

"You don't seem in much of a hurry today. That's great for me. I'm not either."

"Yeh, I ain't in no rush." *Pause.* "He don't normally let me drive it, but he got too much packin' to do, so I'm off to fetch supplies for the long drive tomorrah."

"Drive? What drive?"

"Back to 'Bama."

"What?! You're leaving?"

"Surely am, 'fraid to say."

"You can't be!"

"It ain't up to me," *he said, matter-of-fact.* "Reckon mah folks figger'd that they could drive away from they problems. From they demons, whatever they may be. So they done drove as far north as they coulda without runnin' outta land. Well...it ain't help none. So we headin' back down south again."

"Does...Mary Louise know this?"

"Nuh," *he replied, fishing a loose cigarette out of his front shirt pocket.* "And I'd surely appreciate if you ain't tell her." *He struck a match with his left thumb and lit the cigarette, never taking his right hand from the steering wheel.* "I don't wanna be the ruin of her birthday tonight."

"I understand. I guess."

"We'll talk tomorrah f'sho."

"She really likes you, you know. A lot. It's going to break her heart."

"I don't want that. I truly don't."

"I know. But..."

"Summer wudn't gonna last f'evah any ol' way," *he said, taking a deep drag from his smoke.*

"No, it certainly wasn't."

I couldn't believe it. My heart twinged for how Mary Louise would likely take this news. It wasn't that she didn't know he would be leaving, but just the suddenness of it all...And I tried my best to push from my mind any notion that his sudden departure might somehow be because of me.

"Well...maybe we could come down to Alabama and see you sometime," I said.

He turned quickly toward me then back straight ahead, a baffled, incredulous look on his face that I only saw from my peripheral vision, but still made me feel like an idiot. And I didn't know why.

"Yeah," he chuckled dryly, "if y'all really wanna see me git killed, go right on ahead."

"What does that *mean?*"

"Wow," he replied, shaking his head. "Lord above. You *really* must be from far away, Dya."

"Yes...I am."

"Course, reckon that could happen up here too," he said, pulling into the grocery lot. "Ain't no use in runnin' after all. Eyes are always watchin'. You know whut I mean? Eyes are always watchin'.'"

"I know they are."

I know they are...

We sat in the car in silence for a while. It was a gorgeous day outside. Shoppers bustled past, cotton-white clouds floated up above.

Finally he said...

"You a real nice gal, Dya."

"Thank you."

"I cain't picture you hurtin' so much as a fly."

"I try not to."

"So 'splain it to me then."

"Explain what?"

"Why...why do you feel...dangerous to me? Why you feel like you got a storm chasin' down on you that'll sho' nuff swallow ever'body in its path? How come is that?"

I felt a prickly hot burn around my neck and cheeks. I felt anxious, and angry...but oddly, not angry at him.

"I have no idea what you're talking about, Marvin. That is...just crazy."

"Is it?!" he asked, his gaze off out the window and into the sky. "Is it just crazy talk?"

"Of course it is."

Of course it is...

"How come is it don't nobody know nothin' bout you? Not even Mary Louise really."

"She knows...everything about me. There's just n-not much to know. You know? I've lived a boring life."

"I reckon."

"I have. That's the truth."

"There be somethin'...somethin'...on your trail, m'lady."

"What sort of something?"

"Somethin' dark an' angry an'...savage. I don't know..."

"Oh," I said, trying to sound sarcastic. "That." I don't know if I succeeded or not.

"I don't know what it be...maybe you don't even know your own self..."

"I don't. I really don't."

"But I feel it. And mah instincts ain't often wrong." Pause, and a sigh. "But...maybe they is now. Maybe so. Who can figg'r."

I sat perfectly still, staring at my feet pressed flat against the Pontiac's floorboards, not knowing what to say. Embarrassed and confused. Finally I just said, "I'd better go and get that stuff for the party. Thanks for the ride, Marvin."

"Ain't no trouble." I went to open the passenger side door and he said, "Dya, wait."

"Yes?"

"Just...just promise me somethin', aw'ight?"

"I'll try my best."

THE SONG IN THE SQUALL

"On the off chance that I ain't incorrect, and a damn fool besides, and you actually is runnin' from some kinda wild mess...just promise me...you won't let it git Mary Louise. Whatever it be. Promise me you won't hurt her."

"I would rather die," I said. And I meant it. To the marrow of my bones.

"Your hand on it?" he said, extending his right hand. I knew he expected a standard handshake, but I took it with my left hand instead and placed it over my heart. He shut his eyes and held his breath.

"I would rather die," I said again. He felt my heartbeat, nodded and smiled with an exhale.

"'Kay then."

I got out of the car. As soon as the door was closed I leaned my head down to speak with him one last time.

"See you tonight?" I asked.

"I'll be there with bells on, hear?"

"And Marvin?"

"Yes, m'lady?"

"Don't forget about us, okay?"

And I realize now that what I told you before about him never looking me in the eyes again was imprecise. For in that moment he looked straight at me.

"I don't forget," he said. "I don't never forget."

And with that he drove off.

I moseyed down the road, half in a daze, past all the little shops and vendor carts.

What on earth was that about?!

And no sooner did the thought cross my mind that that had been the weirdest conversation of my life, I felt a cold, firm hand grab me hard around the left bicep.

"Just what in hell do you think you're doing?!" a voice hissed in my ear.

"He's just a friend!" I blurted out without thinking.

I turned around sharply, right there on the street, near a little outdoor café, quite taken aback. There stood a woman, older, well dressed and attractive, but eyeing me up close with a ferocious severity.

"That is not what I mean and you know it!" the woman snarled between her teeth.

"I'm sorry?"

"You heard me, little girl."

She glared, sizing me up from the top of my floppy sunhat to the tips of my pale-pink painted toes.

"Is...something the matter, ma'am?"

I tried to squirm away, but she held all the tighter, her face an inch from mine.

"I know who you are."

I froze. Whatever could she mean?

No one knows who I am. That's impossible.

"I...I'm s-sorry," I stammered, brushing a renegade strand of hair from my face with my free right hand. "You must have me mistaken for someone else. I have to go. People are expecting me."

I tried to pull away, and she squeezed harder. It hurt. My first impulse was to scream as loud as I could, which would likely have caused not just a scene, but actual property damage.

"Oh, I know people are expecting you," she whispered menacingly. "They're likely just now realizing that you've been gone for quite a bit longer than you ought. Can you sense them? Can you feel them coming for you?"

"I don't know what you're talking about!"

"Go ahead. Try to lie to me, little girl. Try to look me straight in the eyes and tell me that you're *not* Kalae's niece."

Leviathan Immortal

January. Portland, Maine. 41.6 inches of snow.
"No need to panic, eh. Everything will be just fine."

They arrived at the vacant storefront at seven o'clock p.m., hauling their equipment through the knee-high snow. Using the raised platform of a front display window for the stage, it was a minor victory to discover that the electricity was in fact on, and all of the outlets were operational.

"*Oh tiny miracles,*" whispered Molly to herself. "*Thank you, tiny miracles.*"

Malik stood in the center of the room and clapped his hands three times. "Acoustics are decent," he said to no one in particular. Dya smiled in spite of herself.

"Hey Dya," Molly shouted over toward her.

"Yeah?!" Dya replied, startled, she quickly returned her eyes to the task at hand: setting up her PA (though not really bothering much with levels and tone, for it was, secretly, just for show).

"How's your foot, eh?"

"Tip top, toes to tendons," Dya answered, her face flushed. *Did she see me looking at him? Does it matter?*

"For real?"

"For real."

"So you don't think your ankle is going to give out and

cause you to fall off the stage? And we'll have to rush you to the hospital a shrieking, bleeding mess?"

"I'm not making any promises."

"That could be kinda wicked, actually," Sarah chimed in. "Brings an air of danger to the show. Pretty metal, eh."

"Well, I'll see what I can do," said Dya. "What should we do with the refreshments?"

"We'll put the coolers in the back," Ethan said. "Food we should set up along that bay of old dryers over there. Don't you think? We'll throw some tablecloths over them and nobody'll be the wiser."

Sarah had "borrowed" two ancient projectors from the AV department at school and set them up at opposing sides of the stage. Perfect for a jittery, grainy ambiance. Behind Malik's drum set she covered the display window with a large white sheet to serve as both a screen and a backdrop.

"Look at it this way, guys," said Malik, tuning his drum heads, "worst case scenario and no one shows, it'll be our first full run of the set accompanied by Sarah's projections."

Everyone attempted, to the very best of their abilities, a hearty affirmation of the sentiment.

8:30 p.m., and they were completely set up, tuned up, geared up and ready. Exactly one half hour before their e-blast said the show would begin.

8:42, and still they were the only ones there.

8:54 and nobody had yet arrived.

9:03. Nothing.

"It's nasty out, eh. Let's hold the curtain just a little longer."

9:10.

9:14.

"Should we just plug in and play anyway? Just for practice?"

"Hmmm…"

THE SONG IN THE SQUALL

* * *

Finally, at 9:22 a single kid came stumbling through the door.

"This the party?" he asked in a congested, shivery voice.

"You're in my study hall, right?" Malik asked.

"Yuh. How's it goin', eh?"

"You're looking at it. You know if...anyone else maybe might be coming? Maybe? Possibly? Anybody?"

The kid just shrugged, pulling off his woolen skullcap and stuffing it into the pocket of his enormous coat. "I wasn't even gonna come, eh. No offense. But, you know, whatever."

"Food's over there. Drinks are in the back. Help yourself."

"Wicked."

The boy trundled off to the grub spread across the dryers, leaving a trail of rapidly melting snow in his wake.

"This is worse than the worst-case scenario," Ethan whispered.

Heartbroken and embarrassed, but not truly surprised, the five were just about to call it yet another hard lesson learned...

When suddenly...and with no warning at all...kids by the dozens began streaming through the door. Looking lost and frozen to the point of disorientation, squinting, though the dim room was lit mostly by colored gels, and trying in vain to shake off the frigid evening air, they peered about the former home appliance discounter as if it were an alien land. Some of these new arrivals the five recognized from school, but many of them were complete strangers.

Immediately assuming the role of hostess, Sarah ran over and welcomed them, very nearly dishing out hugs in the process. Directing them as to where to pile their coats, grab drinks and something to nosh, she turned to the four on stage with a grin and a thumbs-up.

Ethan and Molly strapped on their respective axes as Dya stepped up to the microphone. All the while, more and more people filed in the door.

"Hi everybody," Dya said in a none-too metal fashion. The mic gave a little squeal of feedback. "Thanks for braving the blizzard and coming out to rock with us tonight! This is our first gig. We are Leviathan Immortal!"

Sarah ran up to the front of the stage and switched her projectors on. The words *Leviathan Immortal* appeared on the screen behind them in dripping, slithery letters, greeted by a smattering of random claps.

Ethan began pumping out a sludgy walking bass line. The audience gawked up at the makeshift stage with a dubious mixture of curiosity and befuddlement. But when Malik and Molly slipped in to join him and the insistent kick drum began throbbing like a dragon's heartbeat, a few heads began to bob. Grainy, black-and-white footage of a churning sea swashed across their faces eerily, haunting and foreboding.

The sight and sound was so hypnotic that few barely even noticed that Dya was standing there at the mic (and no one at all noticed when she surreptitiously switched the microphone off). And as such, their shock was all the more absolute when suddenly she split the mounting tension right down the middle with a scream that nearly (and quite literally) knocked them all from their feet.

"*RRRRRRRRRRRRRRRRRIIIIIIIIIIIIIISSSSSSE!!!*"

The song slammed in like a proper explosion, and bobbing heads became banging heads. Folks began to dance...then dance *hard*. And before too long, bodies were colliding this way and that, fists pumped in the air, screaming and hollering. The five looked at each other and smiled in amazement, never missing a beat, continuing to deliver the goods. All along the back of the place people with cell phones began either furiously texting, or holding their camera phones over their heads taking video.

"*RISE UP! FROM DOWN IN THE DEPTHS! RISE UP AND DESTROOOOOOOOOOOOOOOOOOOYYYYY!!!*"

* * *

THE SONG IN THE SQUALL

Twenty-five or so minutes in and another wave of kids came pouring in through the door, obviously hipped to what was going down by those already there. They instantly shed their parkas and dove into the pit, ready to rock the January chill away.

Fifty blistering minutes later, after the band had nearly exhausted their entire repertoire, they kicked into an exuberant (if not entirely note-perfect) medley of Mastodon's "Aqua Dementia," "Seabeast," and "Blood and Thunder," and all in attendance could not help but marvel and wonder as they watched Dya bounce about the stage how such a demonic, inhuman bellow could possibly be coming from such a modestly pretty, but otherwise unexceptional, young girl. And further, as Dya screamed, "*WHITE! WHAAALE! HOLY! GRAAAAAAAAAAAAAAAAAAAAAIL!!!*" folks swore they heard at least three or four different voices screeching and snarling in unholy unison (but, of course that is impossible. Just as the periodic flash of severe emerald that seemed to flash across her eyes must have just been a trick of the green gel light).

In a move of pure rock n' roll showbiz cheese, they closed out the set with an extended chugging vamp and blazing guitar solo courtesy of Ms. Jones on the six-string that had more than one frustrated guitar-slinger in attendance exclaim, "*No one* is that fast on a Les Paul, eh!!!" finally stopping on a dime (more or less) as one.

The crowd burst into a roar of applause.

"Thank you! We are Leviathan Immortal! *Good night!*"

This was greeted by a chorus of protest and chants of—

"PLAY SOME MORE! PLAY SOME MORE! PLAY SOME MORE!"

Dya looked back around to her band mates and they all laughed. Molly stepped up to the microphone and said, "Thank you, but that's all we—what the hell?" Not hearing her voice coming through the PA, she noticed that the mic was switched off. Dya's heart skipped a nervous beat as Molly turned quickly toward her with a quizzical look.

"It feeds back," Dya mouthed to her, thinking fast on her feet. Molly flicked the switch near the mouthpiece and said to their throng of new fans, "Thank you! Thanks for coming out, eh! But sorry, that was all the songs we know!"

"Play them again!" Someone shouted, which was quickly echoed. "Yuh, that's right, you should play them again!" "Some of us got here late, eh!" Someone else hollered. Laughs and further affirmation.

"PLAY SOME MORE! PLAY SOME MORE! PLAY SOME MORE!"

So they did. They played their entire set all over again. It was just that kind of night.

Hours later, after all the food and beverages were gone and the last of the stragglers had finally called it, the five set about cleaning up and packing gear, still flying high from the lingering stage buzz. Dya remembered to affect a limp, and complained some that she "may have overexerted" herself, hoping that it was a convincing enough performance.

"So," Sarah said in what she tried to make a casual tone, "I thought that went pretty all right, eh?"

"Yeah," Malik said, trying his best not to grin ear-to-ear, "it wasn't too terrible."

"Quite good I thought," Ethan chimed in. "Quite good indeed."

No longer able to contain herself, Dya gushed, "Oh you guys...you need to understand...nothing like that *ever* happens where I'm from! *Nothing. Ever.*"

So delirious with adrenaline were they, that none of them even thought to ask her (again) where exactly that might be.

"Nothing like that ever happens anywhere, girlie," Molly said, wiping down the neck of her Les Paul with a clean rag. "It's just one of those things that just doesn't ever happen. But dig; just wait 'til next time, eh. That's when we'll *really* bring the storm."

The following Monday at school, things had largely returned to normal, though there seemed to be a considerable drop in overt hostility aimed at the crew. In fact, coming out of third bell, a small group of kids in the hall whispered to Ethan and Sarah as they passed,
"*Psssst! Wicked show, eh!*"
"Who knows," Sarah said as they continued on, "come graduation, some folks might actually look straight at us."
"Come on now, babe," Ethan deadpanned, "let's not go nuts."
"Stranger things have happened."
And stranger things did.

"Dya! Hey Dya, wait up!"
Dya turned around, and could not believe her eyes. Who should be jogging down the south corridor toward her but Brad Pitre, the handsome rugby player who, along with his buddy Robbo and his girlfriend Trina (of the famous Freak Alert! web page), had threatened her with unspecified harm over the "Jimmie Kendall Incident" back at the beginning of the school year.
What could he possibly want?
"Um...Hi Brad."
"Hey," Brad said, catching his breath. "How's it going, eh?"
Dya looked around. There were only a few other people in the hallway, but Brad did not seem concerned that he might be spotted talking with the likes of her.
"It's going pretty okay I guess."
"So I heard you guys really kicked a whole ton of ass at your

show the other night."

"Yeah," Dya said, still addled by disbelief that the conversation was actually happening. "It was a lot of fun."

"Sorry I missed it."

"Well...we invited you."

"Yuh, I know. But I had a thing. And some stuff."

"Oh. I see."

"So listen," Brad said, with an odd twinge of nervousness in his voice, "I just wanted to say that I'm really, really sorry about all of that crap last fall, eh. I was a total jerkass and I was totally out of line. We all were. And I apologize. You didn't deserve that. You don't deserve that 'Columbine' stuff either."

"N—...nobody deserves it."

"I accept that. I totally do. Absolutely."

What's going on? Is this some sort of prank?

"But anyway," Brad continued, "What I really wanted to talk to you about was...I was wondering, after Spring Break...what are you doing for Spring Break, by the way?"

"We're staying at my friend's cabin. Kind of near Bar Harbor."

"Oh. That's cool, eh. Well, anyhow, after that, after school's back in, they've got this thing...would you be interested in maybe going to the Spring Dance with me?"

Oh my!

Dya was not sure that she wasn't having some sort of hallucination. The hottest boy at school, who prior to this moment had only ever been vicious to her the single time they had interacted (save a brief, wordless encounter near the soccer field)...did he really...just ask her out?

"I...I..."

"*Would love to?* I think that's what you're trying to say,

right?"

"I…I don't…I don't appreciate being tricked, Brad. Or teased."

"What?"

"I saw that movie too, you know. And that's a…a horrible thing to do to a pig."

"It's not like that, Dya. I promise. Hand to God. Seriously, eh. I really want to go with you. I'd really like for you to go with me. It'll be wicked great. Guaranteed. A night to remember!"

"But…why aren't you taking Trina?"

"Ah, we're not really together any more. It's fine and all. I still like her. As a friend. We've just both moved on. Robbo's had his eye on her since freshman year anyhow. They deserve each other, eh."

"I…I don't know."

"Do you like to dance?"

"Sure, I do."

"Do you think it'd be fun to wear a nice dress and eat a fancy meal and drive around in a limo?"

"Um, yes, I think it would. I suppose."

"Has anyone else asked you?"

"No…they haven't."

"Do you think that going to the dance with me might maybe be a slightly better time than staying home with your grandma?" Dya laughed in spite of herself. "Then why say no, eh? Come on."

What would the gang say about this? I'll never hear the end of it!

"You sure you want to go to the dance with a dirty slut?" Dya said with a thin smile.

"Wouldn't be the first time, ha ha ha! Just kidding."

Will they call me a traitor?

"Oh…"

"Come on. Please."

"All…all right. I'll go."

"Wicked," Brad said, and he appeared genuinely thrilled. "It's a date. Let's talk soon, okay?"

Dya nodded silently, her heart slamming in her chest as Brad strolled on down the corridor. Right before heading into a classroom, he turned back toward her and gave a little wave. She returned the wave, but stayed planted in the same spot.

What on earth have I gotten myself into now…

Some Time Ago

"You've been coming up for a while now haven't you," the woman said. I did not reply. I nearly fainted when she mentioned Kalae. "Fallen in love up here, yes? With a person, or just the land itself?" Still I remained silent. "It doesn't matter. Deadly foolishness either way. But tell me. Going back and forth…it's starting to twist you up, isn't it. Feel like your own body is ripping itself apart? Like you're going to die every time you make the change?"

I couldn't help myself. I wordlessly nodded my head. She let go of my arm.

"Let me buy you a drink," she said.

I sipped my cinnamon tea as she very deliberately stirred two large sugar lumps into her coffee.

"I'm still not used to it," she said, unprompted. "I know it's what they drink; coffee. But it's so heavy and bitter on its own."

"I can't handle it," I said, feeling quite the fool, and not sure of what else to say.

The woman continued to stir without another word, for a solid minute. Maybe more. I desperately wanted to run away, but curiosity had me thoroughly affixed to my chair.

Finally she said, "How about a story, Dya."

I had not told her my name. I wanted to ask her how she knew, but instead I simply replied, "All right."

"I'd like to tell you a story of a woman. A young woman from the deep. Stop me if you've heard this one." *But she did not pause for a reply, and continued on.* "This woman, well, she thought herself a woman...but really she was just a naïve girl. A girl who, in a rash and stupid move, decided to give up the deep. Why? For the love of a man. Of course." *She took a deep drink of her well-sugared coffee, and went on.* "For a while she attempted to straddle the two worlds. She would spend time with her man on land, then return to her home in the sea. All was just super-keen for a while...

"But then, she began to get sick. The transformations grew harder. Recovery would take longer and longer every time. Sound familiar?"

"Yes," *I said.* "It does."

"Still, she carried on, attempting to go back and forth between the two worlds. But she began to realize that her body would not be able to withstand the constant transformations much longer. One night, while lying in bed with her man, now her husband, she had a dream. A vision. She saw herself. More specifically, she saw her own death. Her slow, gruesome, agonizing death. She saw what she would become if she attempted to continue as she had been. She saw the twisted, hideous, misshapen creature she was turning herself into, flopping desperately about, gasping for breath, unable to survive in either world."

I gulped hard.

"She had to make a choice," *I said.*

"Yes. Yes I did. I had to make a choice once and for all. You cannot live in both worlds, Dya. You cannot split your time. It's simply impossible. They are both beautiful worlds in their respective ways...but being caught between them is a special kind of hell."

There was a pause as I considered what she had just said. Then finally I replied:

"I've made my choice."

"Have you now?"

"I have."

"And have you considered the full ramifications of that decision?"

"What do you mean? What ramifications?"

"Dya...I can only assume that you have decided to stay on land for good. I can relate. That is precisely what I chose as well. But you must understand, once a certain time has passed...you will never be able to return to the ocean again. Ever. Never again. You will lose the pulse of your people, and they will lose it of you. You will never see your family again. You will never see them again. It will be to them as if you had died."

"And they'll forget me."

"They'd have to. It's part of our survival. Grief must be quick, thoroughly lamented, then forgotten."

"It's supposed to be. But it isn't so always."

"Indeed. Just ask your uncle Kalae about that."

"What do you mean?!"

"I'll never forget the day," she said, looking off toward something vague on the horizon. "In the deepest of the deep. I had not yet met your uncles or your father, though I had heard of them. Our pods were crossing that day, brief but cordial, you know. When suddenly we heard the shrieking, and Kalae came barreling down from above leaving a cloudy red trail of blood from his back, clutching a young land woman's rapidly bloating body to him, calling out to anyone who might hear, 'Help her, please! There must be a way to save her!'"

"What had happened?!"

"I don't know. I don't know any details. Rumors abounded, of course. But all I know was what I saw: your uncle clutching that dead girl's body, his back streaming blood, riddled with bullet holes."

"Oh my god..."

"'Save her! Somebody save her!' He screamed. There was no way, of course. What could anyone do? Everyone was too afraid to approach him, for many reasons, none the least of which was the cloud of blood around him, which was sure to attract sharks. Everyone was afraid...save your father. Someone went to fetch him, and when he finally arrived, he led Kalae and the girl's body away...though I don't know where they went or what was said."

"I didn't know any of that."

"That doesn't surprise me. Your uncle still has bullets lodged in his back, and one at the base of his skull. His body healed around them."

"That...explains a lot about him," I said, more to myself than to her.

"That also does not surprise me."

"It sounds like something right out of one of our old songs," I said, thinking of a few immediately from the top of my head. My hands shook, and I put down my cup for fear of breaking it.

"It does, doesn't it," she replied with a nod. "Those tales and folksongs aren't just stories, Dya. They reflect a long, terrible history. It's a story as old as humanity itself. One of us befriends or falls in love with a person on land, forsakes the sea, and slowly withers and dies in a dry, alien land. Or, a person from the land befriends or falls in love with one of us, attempts to join the world of the deep, and well...you know that end. Centuries upon centuries have passed, Dya, and this has never once been a success. We are simply incompatible, our two people, and we can never be together, no matter how strongly some of us may want to be. Furtive and desperate attempts have only ever ended in tragedy. We must stay apart, separated by fear and folklore and willful ignorance if necessary."

I didn't know what to say. I simply looked at the table.

"You will lose the ability to change," the woman said, moving on. "And, of course, unlike in the deep where life is long...perhaps too long...up here you will age and die like every other land person. Although, as you may have already discovered, aging for us on land is quicker than it is for the natives."

"How much quicker?"

"Almost twice as fast. For every year on land you'll age nearly two."

"Oh..."

"It is almost precisely that. Two for every one."

"That...does answer a few nagging questions."

"Does it?"

"Over the past six years, I've likely spent the overall equivalent of three in the water and three out."

"Dear god, Dya...I'm amazed you're not dead already!"

"Yes...me too..."

"My husband, bless him, born of the land, always a creature of the land, passed on some time ago."

"I'm sorry. He must have been very young."

"They are not strong people, Dya."

"Yes. I know."

"Ten years it's been. And now here I am, all by myself. I am all alone and dying in a world in which I'll never truly belong...or even fully understand."

"I feel very sorry for you."

"I'm not after your pity, Dya, but thank you anyway. I will say this, though. I sure wish I could go home to the deep. It's all I think about. But I simply cannot do it. That is lost to me. Forever."

She finished her coffee, then signaled to the waiter that she would like a refill.

"More tea, madam?" the waiter asked me.

"Yes, thank you," I answered, only half-conscious of my words. My mind swam.

I felt sick for what this strange woman was saying. I did not want to believe it, but I had exactly no reason at all to doubt her.

"Your father," she said, once again stirring a great amount of sugar into her steaming cup. "I just met him the one time. Hardly ideal circumstances, I'll say that. He's quite the...intense individual."

"Aren't they all," I replied. She chuckled. I did a bit as well, just to relieve some of the tension from my chest.

"Indeed. Indeed. Our people...god, I haven't even thought

of them that way in so long...our people, they're a rather primitive lot, aren't they. A feral and aggressive folk by nature. Absurdly secretive and isolationist. Especially the men."

"Is it so absurd though, really?"

"Perhaps not," she shrugged. "I don't blame them for being skittish about the land people. For all their progress, these folks up here sure do make a mess of things."

"There is that, yes."

"I'm sorry if I frightened you earlier, Dya. But once I saw you and realized who you were...I was frightened for you. I mean to say...I know your uncles. I know how they are, and what they are capable of. I have seen it, and it can be terrible. Horrifying. Especially if they think their pod is at risk. They will likely not take kindly to having one of their own abandon the deep for the land, and there may very well be brutal and devastating consequences."

"For whom?"

"Exactly, Dya. For whom indeed. The world of our people is an ancient culture, largely unchanged for many thousands of years. And, like any young immigrant caught between the modern world and that of her people, you have every cause to fear what could happen if these very different worlds were to collide." Her words started my heart to pounding ever harder; so much so that I thought it might explode from my chest and douse the tablecloth with blood. I wondered how well I could heal from something like that. "Think of what that might mean, Dya. Just imagine. Think about how that might someday come crashing down upon those whom you love. Perhaps even sooner than you might think."

I thanked her quickly for the tea, and then tore off down the road and back to Mary Louise as fast as my legs could carry me.

The Secret

"Listen, guys," Mary Louise said, "I'm being completely serious. You can use the cottage, and I don't need to be there. I trust you to use it responsibly...and so forth."

"But we want you to come!" Malik said, and the rest echoed agreement. "Come on Mary Louise, it'll be fun."

"You know you miss the cabin, Mary Louise," Dya said. "Come on."

"Hmm."

"It simply would not be the same without you, dear lady," Ethan said in an exaggeratedly grand fashion.

"You, Mr. Washington, are simply full of baloney," Mary Louise said feigning a cross look and tone that she did not entirely accomplish.

"Perhaps," Ethan replied. "For times are tough and bologna is cheap. But rest assured, that the sentiment is not. Eh."

"Okay okay," Mary Louise said with a resigned sigh. "Count me in. I suppose we can all fit in my car. It'll be pretty snug, though, and it's a solid four hour drive."

"So we can tell our parental units that we're well chaperoned and you'll keep an eye on us and all of that?" Sarah asked.

"You can tell them anything you like, love," Mary Louise answered. "But I have no intention of doing any such thing."

"Precisely," Malik said with a sly grin. "And that's why we love you, Mary Louise. We come for the hospitality; we stay for the benign neglect."

On the drive out to Bar Harbor the lot of them rambled on and on about all of their "big plans" for spring and summer, principally concerning Leviathan Immortal, most of which would likely come of nothing. Still, it was fun to plot and dream. Dya had not yet told anyone of her date for the Spring Dance. Not even Mary Louise. She simply wasn't sure of the best way to bring it up.

One bit of information that she would be sharing with Mary Louise, and only her, as soon as they had a moment alone would be welcome news indeed. For as of that morning, and quite to Dya's surprise, all sense of her people had faded entirely from her. She could not feel them anymore. Not in the slightest. No pulse. No presence. Gone. As if her last bit of tether to the deep had been cut once and for all.

It was a shockingly poignant moment for her, relief mixed with a profound melancholy that she was not quite sure how to share or express. So she opted not to. Instead, she simply hid herself away for a while, and wept.

There is no turning back now. This is it.

Once settled in at the cabin, the six of them drove into Bar Harbor for dinner.

"Touristy, but not tacky" is how Mary Louise described the town. Unanimous consent was that anything would be acceptable for dinner, except lobster.

"No goddamn lobsters, eh. Hideous freakin' things."

Mary Louise pointed out a handful of small clubs to check

out that did not card at the door: something fun for the five of them to do later on without her.

"Didn't you use to live here too, Dy?" Sarah asked.

"Yes, but I really never came into town much."

"Why not?"

Not having an adequate answer to this, Dya and Mary Louise waffled through some opaque nonsense about enjoying the seclusion out at the cottage, which made them sound like they had been in the witness protection program or something, and had sworn secrecy. The subject was finally dropped to no one's satisfaction (or comprehension). By this time Ethan, Molly, Malik and Sarah had grown accustomed to this type of obfuscating from the two of them. And for her part Molly never pressed the issue, assuming as she did, that whatever Dya and her grandmother were keeping from them must be some nasty business indeed.

For the next couple days the gang enjoyed themselves in much the same fashion as they always had back in Portland: blasting their music, watching—and laughing at—gruesome horror flicks (the more gruesome the better), and just generally "bumming around," albeit in a different locale.

"So who, except Dya, would like a beer?"

"Maybe I want one!"

"*Denied.*"

"Forget you then."

Every night they built a bonfire on the shore, talking sometimes until dawn, singing along with some of their very own original songs.

"*Bumbada-bum-bum-bum-bumbada-bum-bum-bum-BONG!*"

"What are you doing, Ethan?"

"Singing my bass line, eh."

"Ah yes."

Free of school, free of the city (fond as they all were of Portland itself), free of whatever intangibles that may have been weighing them down. And, of course, no one felt this unadulterated liberation more than Dya. She was truly on her own now. Free to make herself into the woman she might chose to be, and to cast her fate to the whims of the coastal winds.

And yet, as she sat by the campfire surrounded on all sides by those she loved most in the world, something in her now felt incomplete. (In particular, as she saw Molly's head nestled into the crook of Malik's shoulder, his dreads dangling down across her violet streaks, their fingers intertwined, she could not deny how lonely she was.)

"You know what we should do, eh," Molly said. "When our band gets huge and we're all rich and famous and all? We should all go in on a cottage like this, but even more isolated, and start our own whacked out commune or something."

"An apocalyptic death cult?"

"Is there any other kind?"

Agreement all around.

And then one morning...

"Dya? Pssst, Dya. You awake?"

"I am now," Dya said, rubbing her bleary eyes and trying to focus. "What time is it?"

"Just barely dawn," Molly whispered. "Come on. Let's walk down to the shore. Just you and me."

"Um...really? Now?"

"Yuh now."

"Well...uh...all right, sure."

"You wanna go swimming, eh?"

Oh god...

"You cannot be serious, Moll."

THE SONG IN THE SQUALL

"You know I totally can, dude. Come on. I've seen that look in your eyes when you're near the ocean. You've almost been tempted to come in with me before. I just know it. We'll take a quick dip before everybody else wakes up. It's wicked foggy and awesome out."

I can't...

"Um, well...I...I don't have, you know, a bathing suit or anything."

"I brought two." *Of course you did.* "My extra will fit you."

I really, really can't...

"I'm taller than you are."

"Not by much. Come ooooon."

Bad idea. Bad bad idea.

"I don't know, Moll."

"Then just come walk with me. If you don't want to get in, then you can sit on the rocks and keep me company."

"Hmmm..."

"But, if you change your mind, that'd be wicked awesome."

"Okay. I'll walk with you. But I'm just walking, all right?"

"Yuh, sure thing."

The morning was overcast, misty, and gorgeous. As the fog poured up through the spaces in the rocks like a witch's bubbling cauldron Molly and Dya walked across the flat-stone shore hand in hand for balance.

"Nice, eh?"

"It is."

Once they'd arrived at a sufficiently secluded spot, Molly peeled off her long-sleeved Motorhead shirt and cargo shorts, adjusted her one-piece bathing suit and slid straight into the frigid water below. With a gasp and a hard shudder, she swam out from the rocks.

"How is it?" Dya asked, looking out across the rippled ocean surface sprawling before her, her body trembling with desire.

I am never going to shake this need...

"It's the best ever, eh!" Molly shouted back. "You'd live a thousand years if you did this every morning, Dya! I promise you that!" *You don't say.* "You don't know what you're missing, girlie!"

If only you knew...

Molly proceeded to dive under and pop up again with a splash, kicking her legs in the air, singing David Gray at the top of her voice.

"*Sail away with me honey / I put my heart in your hand / Sail away with me honey now / now / now...*"

"I'd get in," Dya said, "but I don't want to put the suit on out here where people might see me!"

"Dya, there's no one around for five miles at least. Nobody's gonna see you. Hell, just come in in your skivvies. I promise I won't tell, eh." And she continued to sing—

"*Crazy skies are wild above me now / winter howling at my face / and everything I held so dear / disappeared without a trace...*"

Out further, barely visible from where she stood, Dya saw a large boulder jutting out from water, which crashed white and foaming around it. Lying across it in great heaps were harbor seals barking and calling, simply to hear the sound of their own voices. Coming within fifty yards of the seals was illegal in these parts, and they seemed to know it, confident that they could go about their business undisturbed.

"Shush," Dya said under her breath and the seals instantly fell silent (though one clearly grumbled in protest). She smiled with great affection for them, though of course they could not see it.

Finally she could stand it no longer.

I can't make my peace with life on land if it is going to be like this forever...

This is it...This is the test...can you touch...can you touch the water and still keep your legs? Only one way to know...

THE SONG IN THE SQUALL

So, fighting against every bit of better judgment she possessed, Dya pulled off her clothes down to her bra and underwear and dove straight in.

Oooooh my...Oh my yesssss...

Hitting the piercing cold of the sea, Dya thrilled to her true environment at long last. Diving down deep she caressed the rocky floor, tasting the chilled brine on her lips, spinning in a corkscrew motion, whipping her long auburn hair through the water like it was a strong gust of wind.
Must keep my feet, though...I have to keep my feet...
Popping up to the surface, she heard Molly cheer.
"Right on, dude!" Molly shouted, gasping for breath through cold-constricted lungs, "See, I *knew* you were a badass chick, eh!"
"You're always right, Molly," Dya replied with a bright smile. She took a deep, shuddering breath, back flipped, and dove back down again.
Overjoyed as she was to finally be back in the water again after a long year away, the struggle to keep her land body was disturbingly difficult. Almost as if her legs, of their own will, wanted to come together and fuse as one. As if they yearned to be—
No! No, fight it...fight it...
"Molly...can I...tell you something?"
Fight it...you must...
"Sure thing, eh!"
Don't give in!
"You're my best friend, Molly," Dya said. "You're my best friend in the whole world. After Mary Louise, of course."
Molly just laughed.
"Mary Louise is your grandma, weirdo!"

"Right…right," Dya said, she felt her mind clouding, as if the water was making her delirious. *So this is aqua dementia…Focus, damn it!* "That's what I mean. That's why you're my best friend."

"Right back atcha, dude," Molly said with a wink and a smile, as she ventured out further into deeper water.

Tell her…she has a right to know…

"Molly?"

Show her…

"Yuh?"

"Can you…swim in closer to me?"

"Um…sure!"

No more secrets…no more games…

"There's something I want to share with you," Dya said directly.

Molly swam toward Dya with great interest.

"Okay?"

Treading water very near one another, they bobbed in the waves, face to face.

"I can trust you, right Molly?"

"What?"

"Promise me I can trust you, Molly."

Still treading water, Molly faced Dya head on. Quizzical. Curious. Dya looked at her with an intensity Molly had never seen before. Her eyes seemed to have changed somehow. The soft hazel was a bit harder now. Sharper. A more piercing green. Like they were slowly becoming cut jewels. Emeralds. It frightened Molly a little. And intrigued her.

"Promise me, Molly. Please. Please tell me I can trust you."

Molly felt herself oddly hypnotized by Dya's changing eyes. She didn't know what to make of this new side of her friend.

"Of course you can, Dya. Of course you can. I'm sorry to laugh earlier. You're my best friend too, eh. You can tell me anything."

No more lies…no more foolishness…

"Not so much a 'tell,' Molly," Dya said. Even her voice seemed different. More ethereal. More resonant. "It's something I want to *share* with you."

"Oh."

"Something I've only ever shared with one other girl. A long, long time ago. But I want to share it with you too."

"Wow...Um...Okay..."

"I really like you, Molly. I really care about you, and I want to share this. But if you don't think—"

"No, no," Molly interjected. "I want to. I definitely want you to. Whatever it is."

"Better head into the shallow water then," Dya said. "So your feet can touch bottom."

"So it's like that, eh?" Molly tried to laugh. Dya did not.

"Yes it is," Dya replied simply. "It is like that."

"Okay sure," Molly said, and swam back closer to the rocky shoreline.

"Close your eyes, Molly."

"All right."

Dya took a deep breath, dove under, slipped out of her undergarments, and closed her eyes.

Immediately she felt the change. Her feet stretched thin, growing together into flukes; her cold, pink legs became warm and sleek, shimmering silver, fusing as one. With a flash she shot out into deeper water.

Faster and faster she barreled through the water, simply because she could. The burn of a short, hard breath eased in her lungs, and at once she felt as though she could now stay submerged for many months. For indeed she could. And she very much wanted to. But there were other matters to address at the surface.

Breaking through into the air above she inhaled greatly again, dove back down and shot in, allowing her tail to propel her back toward the shore.

There in the shallower water, shoulder-deep, stood Molly.

Her eyes still closed. Waves splashing up on her face intermittently. Her head cocked to the side, her lips slightly pursed. Dya caressed her friend's cool, damp cheek. Molly smiled and opened her eyes.

Surprised as she was at first by the sight of Dya nude from the waist up, it was nothing to her shock when she saw Dya beneath the surface of the water, silver and sleek, tossing back bright beads of what little sunlight shown above.

For a moment there was silence, but for the splashing waves. Molly could simply not trust her poor, weak eyes. Then Dya brushed against Molly's bare leg underwater with her smooth, shimmering tail.

And Molly screamed. Like she had never in her life screamed before.

"Molly!" Dya screamed as Molly clawed her way out of the water and ran, hysterical, back down the rocky beach.

Catch her! Catch up to her!!!

Dya grabbed the nearest jutting rock and hoisted herself from the sea onto the pebble beach, combat-crawling up the stones, dragging her lower half behind her. She concentrated with all of her strength to bring back her legs and feet so that she could chase after Molly...

...but she could not make it happen.

"Oh, come on! *Come on!*"

Her legs refused to come. Refused to cooperate. As she lay in shallow water, the waves crashing and receding over her exposed tail she shut her eyes tightly, focusing on nothing but the change to her land form. To no avail. All the while losing precious time.

"*Molly please!*" she cried. "*Please come back!*"

Finally, as the clouds above broke and spangles of sunlight danced across her glistening silver skin, she felt her tail spilt down the middle at last. The pain was sudden, unexpected, and excruciating. As if she were being attacked simultaneously with lye and a dull axe. Silver faded to burning pink, blotched with red from the cold and the pebbles, bones grew hard where there had been none, toes and feet formed from thin flukes. She screamed out for the agony of it all.

Back to the state she had held for the past year, she stood unsteadily, grabbed her jean shorts and windbreaker from the boulders. She dressed quickly, then broke into an awkward, haphazard, barefoot sprint down the stony shore, frantically calling Molly's name.

"*Molly! You promised!!!*"

One Last Time

"YOU PROMISED!" she sobbed, chasing me down the beach, Marvin following quickly behind us, though keeping his distance so as not to intrude. "You promised you were staying!"

"I know!" I cried, tears scalding my face. "But there are some things I...I...I need to deal with first!"

"But why?!?! What are they?!?! Why do you have to leave now?"

I jabbered some hysterical madness about tying up loose ends, saying final goodbyes or something...and in the process I let something slip about violent repercussions if anyone were to come looking for me. I did not want to say that...I absolutely did not want to frighten her...I simply could not help myself.

She stopped dead still in the white sand.

"Wh—what kind," she sobbed through heaving breaths. "What kind of violent repercussions?"

"I don't know, Mary Louise! That's what I need to find out! I have to be sure you'll be safe!"

"Why would I not be safe?!"

"I will not let anything hurt you."

"I'm fine, Dya!" she cried. "I'll be just fine! You don't have to—"

"You don't know my people! You don't know what they are capable of!"

And neither did I.

THE SONG IN THE SQUALL

I nearly stepped straight into the water without a look back, when she screamed behind me.

"Dya, wait!"

I turned around, and we threw our arms around each other, clinging desperately and sobbing into the other's shoulders. Up the beach a bit I saw Marvin standing by awkwardly, and I felt for him, how confusing this all must have been. We had just met, after all. He had no idea of who I was other than "Mary Louise's friend." And here I stood, by all appearances intending to stomp off into the ocean, and into a watery grave. Whatever dark suspicions he had about me were certainly validated that day. For they were valid.

Although at least I suppose I rendered his own bad news for her less terrible by comparison.

"I promise. I promise I'll come back," I whispered into her ear. "Feel my heart. I promise on my life. I'll come back. And when I do, it will be forever."

"But when?!?" she cried. "When will that be?"

"Soon," was all I could say in return. "It'll be soon."

"Don't go...please...please..."

I brushed her tear-streaked hair away from her damp, blotchy face and kissed her cheek. "I love you," I said, and turned to run head-on into the sea.

"Dya, what you doin'?!" I heard poor Marvin yell as my head went underwater, his sneakers pounding into the sand as he ran down the beach toward us. "Come on back here!"

I don't know what she ever told him about what happened that day. That day they saw me disappear into the chopping waves at Ogunquit...and then not return. I don't know what she told her parents when I wasn't there for the party.

Or ever again.

All I knew was that I had to get back to the deep. That, whatever may come next, I simply was not yet ready to give up forever all that I that had ever known. I needed to think hard about so drastically shortening my life. And once I did commit to the land once and for all, which I truly wanted to do, which I *had promised that I would, I had to feel reasonably sure that I could cut the line to my people. That I would not be followed. And furthermore, I simply had to see the deep one last time. To bask in its frigid glory. To thrill once more to the bioluminescent beauty, and the great calm of the bottomless dark. To say a final goodbye to my life, and the girl that I had been.*

And I did just that, Molly. I spent my time. I weighed the severity of what it all meant. Do you understand?

When the Family Comes To Call

She found her at last, huddled on the ground in nothing but her bathing suit in a stand of white birch, shivering and rocking, her chin pressed tight against her knees.

They stared at one another in silence for a long while, neither knowing quite what to say.

Finally, Dya broke the stillness as best she could.

"Are you...all right?"

"Who are you?" Molly asked softly.

Dya's heart shattered into a thousand pieces. She sat down on the ground opposite Molly.

"I'm Dya, Molly. The same Dya you've known for the past year."

"Like hell, eh."

"I am! I'm Dya! Your friend!"

"Yuh, okay."

"Is it?"

"It is."

"Are you sure?"

"Of course." Pause. Then, "I always...I always kinda maybe felt that there was something fi—something strange about you, Dya. I always felt there was something."

"I thought strange was good."

"It is," Molly replied in a hush. "It is good."

"But..."

"But nothing. I mean…okay. You…you are…you are a freakin' mer—"

"*Don't say that word!*" Dya yelled, louder than anyone should reasonably be able to. Molly covered her ears, startled, pressing her back hard against the bark of the white birch behind her, her eyes like saucers. "I am not that…*thing*! That made-up thing! I'm not a fairytale. I'm a human being. *My people are human*, and land people have never made their peace with that. They've never understood. So they made us the…stuff of legends. Said we were half-fish, or ancient god creatures, or magical nymphs or other such nonsense. But I'm none of that. I'm a girl, a regular girl, just like you! I'm just…from somewhere else. That's all."

"Where are you from?"

"I'm…"

"Where are you from, eh?!"

"I'm from…" Dya exhaled. "I'm from the deep. The deepest end of the ocean."

"Oh god…" Molly cried, burying her face in her hands. "Oh my god…"

Dya did not know what to do. She sat in the dirt and silently watched her friend cry and shake her head in disbelief, all the while a creeping despair and humiliation enveloped her. Dya lowered her head as hot tears began to sting her eyes and fall softly into her lap.

"I thought…I thought I could trust you…"

Suddenly, Molly's head snapped up. Like a hungry cat pouncing on its prey Molly leapt toward Dya from a sitting position. She grabbed Dya's face with both hands and, for a moment, Dya nearly thought Molly was going to bite her. But instead, she pressed her forehead against Dya's and stared straight into her hazel-emerald eyes.

"*Teach me*," she whispered.

"What?!"

"Teach me to be like you." Her voice was desperate, pleading, but direct. Insistent. "I want to do what you can do. It's what I've always wanted. What I've always dreamed of."

"Molly, I—"

"I don't believe in god, Dya. I don't believe in anything. But my whole life, since I was a very little girl, I prayed for this day. Do you understand that? I dreamed and wished and hoped and prayed with all my heart and soul. I prayed that someday you would come, and take me away...to the deepest end of the ocean. And...and now...you're here at last! *At last*. Please teach me how. Please."

"You prayed that *I* would come?"

"I didn't know that it would be *you*. I just dreamed that someday...that she would be a m—a misfit like me, and she would come to me, and we would swim off to a whole other world beneath the sea."

"Molly...I...I can't teach you—"

"*Why not?!*"

"I...I just don't know how! I don't know that it's possible!"

"But you said we are the same, eh!" Molly said, nearly shouting, her lips tight and down-turned. "You said you're a regular girl like me! So if you can...!"

"Molly, I...My people...We just evolved this way. We remained in the sea when half of our common ancestors, *your* ancestors, moved to land. We evolved in a different way. And you evolved the way you did." Molly let go of Dya and plopped back down onto the ground opposite her, listening intently, not ready to give up easily.

"My people..." Dya continued, "we need to be able to change and adapt immediately to a variety of...constantly changing circumstances. Rogue waves...white squalls...extreme shifts in water pressure, and temperature...not to mention dangerous predators...we have to be able to adapt to it all. It's crucial for our survival. If we couldn't adapt on the fly, we would have perished long ago. I just...I don't think it's possible to cram hundreds of thousands of years of evolution into a couple of days over Spring Break."

Molly looked absently off into a random, adjacent thicket. Neither spoke for quite a while as the full scope of the situation unfurled before each of them individually. The silence between them hung thick and oppressive.

"What a rip-off, eh," Molly said finally.

Dya couldn't help but smile sadly. "I came up here…because I wanted to be like *you*."

Molly laughed bitterly.

"Why would anybody want to be like me."

Dya leaned in toward her, and said very intently, "In the year that I've known you, Molly, in this time that I've spent with you, I've experienced more of life than I had in the fifty-one years since I was last on land. So much more. More than I could ever say. In this past year, what you think was just a bunch of nothing, was a hundred lifetimes to me."

"I don't think it was nothing."

"I'm glad for that."

"Fifty-one years…Jesus…"

"That's right. Fifty-one years in the deep. I hadn't even realized. Time loses all meaning down there. And for all the wildness of the environment…the culture has not changed a single iota in thousands and thousands of years. Same rote tales, same static history, same never-ending, meaningless traditions."

"How…how old are you, Dya?"

"I don't really know. Mary Louise figures I'm about ninety-eight years old. She likes to keep up on that sort of thing, for some reason."

"God. Ninety-eight."

"So far as we can tell."

"And that's…young, eh?"

"Quite a bit younger than you are right now. Comparatively speaking."

"Mary Louise…she isn't your grandma."

"No. She isn't. She's a pretty little girl I shared a secret with years and years ago."

"That's crazy, eh."

"I suppose. It doesn't feel crazy, though."

"So, okay. Tell me then. What's it like down there?"

"It's...beautiful. Endlessly beautiful. Cold and dense. But I like that."

"Me too."

"I know."

"And dark I bet? Pitch black?"

"It is, in parts. But, depending upon where you are, it can be teeming with bioluminescence. Anglerfish. Black dragonfish. It's quite gorgeous, actually. And rather bright in its way."

"That sounds wicked amazing."

"But...you know what they don't have down there?"

"What?"

"Peaches."

"Peaches?"

"No peaches and cream. No strawberries. No chocolate. No bananas and custard."

"I'm pretty sure I could live without peaches, eh."

"You might think so," Dya said. "But I don't think I can. Not anymore. Not once you've tasted a really good one. And you'd miss things you didn't think you would. And people most of all."

"Don't you miss your family down there?"

Dya looked out through the stand of birch and squinted at the sunlight as it finally began to break through. Although it wasn't visible, they could hear the ocean crashing against the shore.

"Yes. I do. It's funny, but even in the deep it's been a very long time since I've seen my parents. They went off to visit friends or other relatives in other parts of the sea. I don't even remember why they left. It has been many, many decades since they departed, and underwater I barely give them a thought. But I miss them now. I wonder about them and where they are and if they're okay. That only happens on land. It's weird."

"Why don't you try to find them and then come back, eh?"

"I can't. Bad things will happen."

"What exactly would happen?" Dya did not answer, but her silence said, *Something truly awful*. "Dya," Molly continued, "I honestly think I could give up all this bull crap, eh. Cell phones, reality TV, whoopie pies, high school, I'd be rid of it all without too much difficulty. Right now. I could even stand never seeing my dad and my jailbird brother ever again, to tell you the honest truth."

"What about Malik? What about Ethan and Sarah?"

"Yuh," Molly admitted with a nod, "that would be wicked hard."

"Okay...Could you give up your guitars?"

"What?"

"Instruments don't work down there."

"None at all? Not even, like, sea drums or anything?"

"There's no sludge metal in the deep, Molly."

Molly turned and faced Dya. They both smiled.

"Well...sucks to that then, eh."

They laughed. And then they laughed harder. Harder than was likely called for, but it was a relief to do so.

"Although," Dya said, "I should say, some of the music of the deep isn't really quite so different as you might think. Some of our songs are sweet, lilting lullabies."

"Like that song you sang in the woods!"

"Some are like that. And some are vicious, shrieking murder ballads. It swings pretty wide."

"I bet I'd love it," Molly said hungrily. "I'd love it all."

Dya put out her hands, and Molly took them in hers.

"But see," Dya said, "that I *did* bring up with me. That I *can* share with you."

"And..." Molly said, her eyes twinkling with the light of a grand new design, "so long as we keep it a secret, and maybe made new lyrics, we could share it with the world, eh."

"I don't see why not."

THE SONG IN THE SQUALL

Molly's face lit up for the first time since they'd left the water. She seemed positively giddy at the idea of bringing the music of the deep to land, at least in some form. Sounds that no living person on two legs had ever heard...and survived.

"Dya...you have to tell the others."

Dya sighed, and then nodded her head.

"I will. I will. I promise. Just...not yet."

"Well, you have to tell Malik at least. Or I'll have to."

"Why?"

"Because he and I never keep secrets from one another. Not ever."

Hmmm...Are you so sure of that?

"Okay," Dya said, fully committed. She felt oddly relieved by Molly's insistence. As if it lifted a bit of the burden from her shoulders alone. "I'll tell him. Before we head back to Portland. I'm not going to show him, though. I can't do that. Ever again. I can't go in the ocean. It's too painful."

"Tonight. You need to tell him tonight, eh."

"Tonight?"

"Don't worry. I'll be there with you. I'll support you."

Dya gulped. "All...all right. Tonight."

"So," the grocery lady said, her practiced smile chiseled into her face with no small amount of discomfort, "you folks in Bah Hah'bah long, eh?"

Molly could not help but smirk a bit. The subtext of the lady's question could not have been more clear—*We appreciate you outsidahs' dollahs, but we want yo'ah outsidah asses gone with all due speed.* She glanced over to Malik and Dya next to her to see if they had caught the lady's vibe as well. If they had, it did not show. They were too busy bagging up their great pile of pretzels, ice cream, and frozen pizzas into cloth sacks.

In fairness to the grocery woman and her none-too-subtle xenophobia, Molly thought, the three of them did stand out from the local crowd just a bit. But for her demon-emblazoned *High On Fire* T-shirt, Dya was not particularly eye grabbing...for Malik and herself, however, the same could not quite be said.

Folks might take notice...what can you do...

"No," Molly replied, pulling money out of her studded black Infectious Threads purse, "just here for Spring Break. We're staying outside of town a ways."

"Ayuh," the woman said, taking the money with the same forced grin. "In from Mass-of-two...um...er...uh...Massachusetts? Sorreh."

"We're from Portland, eh," Molly answered, a hint of annoyance slipping through her voice. The woman's face relaxed slightly. Portland is still Maine at least.

"Ayuh, Pah'tland's a fine town. Lived the'ah m'self a shah't while back in college. A fine town."

"Yuh, it's good," Molly said, collecting her change. She, Malik and Dya grabbed their bags of snacks and sodas and various munchables.

"You folks have a pleasant stay, eh."

"Thank you. We shall."

On the drive back to the cabin, Dya and Malik both said they had completely missed the vibe of being overly profiled by the checkout lady at the grocery, much to Molly's exasperation.

"You guys just aren't sensitive to that crap like I am, eh," she said. Malik and Dya both chuckled for the irony.

Once back to the cabin and pulling up the gravel, Molly said, "Mal, you think you could bring the stuff in and meet Dya and me down by the water?"

"Um...okay?"

"There's something the three of us need to discuss. Just the three of us. For now."

"Th...there is?"

Malik glanced over toward Molly in the passenger seat with a look of panic in his eyes.

"Remember, Moll," Dya said urgently from the back seat. "We can talk about it, but I can't—"

"I know, I know."

Without another word, Malik shut off the car engine, grabbed the grocery bags, and dutifully carried them off to the house, his limp compounded only slightly by the additional weight of the bags.

I'll bet he thinks I told about the kiss, Dya thought, and wanted to find the misunderstanding funny. But she was simply too nervous laugh, trying to think of a way to properly explain her "situation" to Malik without actually showing him. Molly's eyewitness support would likely be of little help, and her initial reaction had rendered Dya more than a bit gun shy.

He'll just think we're both crazy...or playing some kind of dumb joke.

Dya and Molly walked along the pebbled beach hand in hand, watching the perfect round moon cast its reflection across the vast ripples of the ocean. Dya felt herself resenting the gorgeous crash and churn of the waves against the rocky shore. Like it was mocking her.

"I'll be the one to tell him if you want, eh," Molly said.

"He won't believe you any more than he will me," Dya replied. "I certainly wouldn't if I were him."

"It doesn't matter. I just want him to know. I don't want to be the only one who knows. I don't want secrets between us. Any of us."

"I don't either. I just...don't know what to say."

They looked up the beach to see Malik ambling down toward them with invisible weight on his shoulders, clearly in no hurry to get there.

"So," said Malik as he reached them finally, "a moonlight stroll along the beach with two fine ladies." He gave them a broad, and somewhat desperate, smile. "Whose ass did I save in a previous life to earn me this pleasure, huh?"

Molly took his hand and squeezed it tight.

"Mal?"

"Yeah, homie, what up?"

"We've known each other a long time, eh."

"Sure have, babe. We sure have." His voice seemed to betray more than a touch of panic.

"And I really care about you a lot," Molly continued, letting go of Dya's hand and taking Malik's other hand as well. "Even before we were…you know…*together*-together, I always felt like I could confide in you about anything and everything. I've always felt that. Even if the rest of the world had turned their back on us, between you and me, between Malik and Molly, there was nothing but truth, eh. Always. We're strong together like that."

"Mmmm hmmm." Malik nodded his head more vigorously than necessary. "Yeah, that's right, babe." Even in the cool breeze of the evening, sweat beads began to break on his forehead, and he swallowed hard.

"So, with that in mind," Molly went on, "Dya shared something with me today that I…didn't want to just stay between the two of us. And, before you say anything, I know for a fact that it's all true, eh."

"Look, y'all," Malik said, his tone now strangled and reedy, his natural (though oft-suppressed) down-South twang rising slightly to the surface, "I think I know what this's all about, a'ight, and let me just come on right out n' go ahead n' say—"

"MAL!" Dya interrupted. Malik stopped cold, his mouth still open. Dya shook her head and made a cutting motion across her throat. Dya watched as the look on Malik's face morphed oddly from guilt and panic, to distraction, to confusion, to something resembling terror...and she realized too late that he was not looking at her, but beyond her, toward the sea.

"What..." Malik whispered, "what in holy hell is tha—"

In a flash, Dya's entire field of vision was filled with blinding white light as a searing pain collided with the back of her head.

She fell hard to the pebbles, all around her a hideous snarling and shrieking could be heard...and amongst the dissonant alien caterwauls, the unmistakable sound of Molly—though not Malik—crying out in fear and pain.

"Thought we'd lost you, Dya," a rattling voice croaked. "Lost all sense of you. Thought you were dead. Until this morning. And suddenly, there you were again."

Dya panicked, still unable to see, frightened not so much from the angry gurgling sounds echoing around her as she was by the fact that she could hear Molly screaming—

"*Don't touch him! Leave us alone!*"

Shaking off the blindness and the pain in the base of her skull, Dya's eyes cleared enough to see Malik slumped to the ground, bloody and barely conscious. Molly lay next to him crying, bleeding from the corner of her mouth, attempting to shake him awake, swinging her free arm wildly in the air to ward off unseen attackers. Dya could no longer make out what Molly was saying. All she could decipher amidst the swirling cacophony of shrieking and hissing was the vicious, growling voice of her uncle.

"What have you done, you stupid, careless, selfish girl..."

"Kalae please," Dya gasped, still recovering from whatever had struck her from behind. "These are my friends!"

Her vision fully restored at last, she stared straight into her uncle's piercing, frozen sapphire eyes. He glared back at her through great, drenched ropes of silver hair, nearly vibrating with rage, seething breaths heaving and sucking through his bared teeth, his rippling arm and chest muscles flexing and releasing involuntarily beneath taut, glistening wet alabaster skin.

She had never seen him with legs, of course, and the sight left her momentarily dumbstruck. His legs, however recognizable as such in a broad sense, glistened silver in the moonlight, alien and aquatic in appearance, as if he had refused to degrade himself with a full transformation to land.

"Friends?" he hissed, grabbing Molly and Malik by their respective collars, and lifting them up. Molly cried out, but was quickly stifled by the pressure of her shirt collar against her throat. Malik's eyes rolled back as his head flopped about unconscious, convulsing from a hard drop in blood pressure. "Which of these dirt creatures is the one you are willing to abandon, disgrace and endanger your people for? Speak quickly! I have business with the one whom you love most."

By the angry hissing and gurgling slithering ever closer at her back, Dya knew what was creeping up behind her: a flank of wild, naked men, bone white and shimmering silver, ready and hungry for violence, no doubt hand-picked by Kalae to join him on this adventure for their muscle and aggression.

Quite against her will, Dya's eyes involuntarily flashed toward the cottage a short distance up the small hill, nestled just off the beach line and back into the trees. In an instant, Kalae let go of Molly and Malik and they fell to the ground again. He screeched and clicked toward the row of ocean men encroaching upon Dya and they all went barreling off in the direction of the house.

"No! *Stay away!*" Dya screamed, knowing full well of its utter futility. "They've done nothing wrong!" She shrieked and jabbered at them in a foreign, underwater tongue, but they ignored this as well.

Dya pulled Molly to her feet. Molly screamed, "What are those things?!?"

"They're my uncles. And they are very, *very* dangerous! We have to get to the others!"

The two of them managed to hoist Malik up between them and drape each of his arms over their shoulders. Regaining enough consciousness to move his legs well enough to walk without being dragged, Malik was still bleeding heavily from his face, and jerking with hard muscle spasms. As quickly as they could, the three hurried frantically up toward the cabin, praying it was not too late.

As beautiful and graceful as they may have been under water, Dya's uncles appeared nothing but brutish and inelegant as they lumbered ahead of them toward the cottage on awkward new legs, all the while chattering to one another in ugly whines, clicks and growls. The counter-intuition it required of Molly to chase after them was nearly impossible to sustain.

Miraculously, though, the men stopped just short of the porch, waiting, more or less at attention. They fanned out, surrounding the cottage on all sides. Even more strangely, they allowed Dya, Molly, and Malik access unobstructed, though not before one of them extended a right hand of sharpened silver fingernails and slashed at them ferociously. Dya wailed as her left forearm ripped open, blood spurting across Molly's right cheek.

"*Dya!*" Molly screamed in horror.

"I'm okay!" Dya replied, her voiced clipped from the pain. "Let's get inside!"

As they entered the cabin, Molly looked to her right just in time to see the angry, bleeding gouges in Dya's arm seal up into the mere faintest of scratches.

Stepping into the kitchen, they found Sarah and Ethan pressed hard against the wooden cabinets, their eyes wide and terror-struck.

"*There's something in here!*" Sarah whispered, quaking and choked with fear.

"Dya'sss fam'ly payin' a visssit..." Malik slurred through bloody lips, just barely keeping his head steady. "Don' go ou'side 'less you wanna die in a real nasty kinda way..."

Unable to resist, Ethan peeked out the window to see the throng of growling, seething ocean men staring back, waiting for a signal or a reason to charge in and tear them all to pieces.

"What the goddamn..." he gasped in horror. "This...can't be real, eh."

As if on cue, Kalae entered the kitchen, heavy and deliberate in his footsteps, his large, powerful left hand wrapped firmly about Mary Louise's throat.

"NOOOOOOOOOOOOOOOOOO!!!" Dya screamed so loudly the glass rattled in the windowpanes and a spice rack crashed to the floor. Everyone save Kalae tensed and shut their eyes for the violence of the sound. "YOU LET HER GO NOOOOOOOOOOOOOOOOOOOOOOOW!!!"

Mary Louise's eyes were glassy with fear, shifting around this way and that, though her face remained oddly still. Even stoic. As if she had been steeling herself for the inevitability of this moment for quite some time.

"You brought this," Kalae croaked at Dya. "You've shamed your family and endangered your kind. And now these poor animals will all need to be destroyed because of you."

Sarah gasped and covered her mouth. She buried her face in Ethan's shoulder, who looked equally terrified.

"You'll not hurt them!" Dya shouted. "Just leave us alone!"

Kalae's already furious face contorted in rage.

"*Us? Us?!?!* The only 'us' for you is standing outside, Dya, waiting to collect you and take you home."

"*This* is my home now! I've chosen the land! It's my right to do so!"

"Don't speak to me of your 'rights.' I promised your father I would mind you until his return."

"He's never going to return, Kalae! Neither is my mother. Nor any of my brothers or sisters. None of them are. And I don't care, because I don't care to ever see them again. I'm not coming back either."

With that, Kalae wrapped his other hand around Mary Louise's throat as well. She closed her eyes, but did not flinch.

"You realize you are killing her right now."

"NO!"

"It's your choice."

"If you so much as leave a scratch on her, Kalae," Dya said, her eyes burning wild and savage, "I will…"

"Yes? You will…?"

"You want to force me back to the deep…fine. Okay. Fine. Just let her go. Please. Let her go and then I will go back down with you. But I swear…I swear…"

"You swear what, stupid girl?"

"*Resurgam*," she hissed under her breath.

"I think not," he hissed in reply. "Not so long as I am alive."

"Then I will make every moment of the rest of your miserable life a perpetual torment!"

Kalae chuckled coldly. "It already is." He released Mary Louise from his clutches with a rough push. Dya moved to run to her, but Kalae put out his hand to stop her.

"Please, Kalae," Dya said, tears streaming down her face. "Please let my friends go."

"Even if I wanted to, which I don't, I could not," he gurgled in reply. "Too risky. I know only too well what destruction these dirt creatures are capable of. They have to die. All of them. Thanks to you."

Sarah wailed, holding ever harder to Ethan, as if there was anything he could do about their present situation. Molly stood silently stroking Malik's dreadlocks as he slumped against her, bleeding down the left leg of her faded blue jeans.

"Kalae, listen to me," Dya cried. "That is my dear friend Mary Louise standing there next to you. And this is Molly. And Ethan. And Malik. And Sarah. I love them all so much. They're not creatures. They are human beings, just like we are. And they have families and friends who love them very much and will be *very* upset if they don't return."

Nice bluff, Dya, Molly thought. *I hope he believes it. Good thing he doesn't actually know us.*

"And anyway," Dya continued, "if you think it's too much of a risk to leave them alive to tell a tale, just think of what would become of our people in the deep if those same families and friends come seeking revenge. You know they can. And they will. They have oxygen tanks. And pressurized ships that can drop all the way to the ocean floor. And *guns*. Our people would be no match. The others back home might not know that...*but I know you do*."

At the mention of ships and guns, panic flashed across Kalae's sapphire eyes. He rubbed the back of his head reflexively, long white fingers entangled in silver.

"I'm not a cruel man," Kalae growled, then stepped back away from Mary Louise. She did not move one way or the other, and continued to stand still, her face a solid, impassive mask. "But you must know that this is impossible. This cannot stand." He turned to Mary Louise and spoke directly to her for the first time. "Do you know what will happen to her if she remains on land past the point where she can no longer return to her proper form?"

"No," Mary Louise replied, so quiet as to be nearly imperceptible.

"She will dry out, wither and die...just like you, *dirt hag*. And much sooner than you have at that." He turned to the four young ones and said, "As each of you age year by year, she will do so twice as quickly. You will barely be entering into your adulthood and she will be wrinkled, worn and graying."

Ethan, Molly, and Sarah stared back in dumb shock. Malik stirred awake, but did not appear to comprehend. Only Mary Louise looked truly startled by this news.

"That's my choice!" Dya yelled angrily. Kalae ignored her, and continued to address her friends instead.

"Giving up a long life of health, strength, youth, beauty, freedom...all of the ocean is hers with virtually no borders or obstacles...and she's to give all that up? Just to get old, decrepit, and frail like the lot of you. Would you wish that upon her?"

"It's *my* wish, Kalae!" Once again, Dya's pitch threatened to crack the windows for its force. "It's my life!"

"Why can't she jusss...go to the ocean for a while and then come back?" Malik asked, at last fully conscious, though still struggling to focus. He did not appear the slightest bit timid about asking this strange, naked sea man a question point-blank. He had already been assaulted, after all, and figured there was no use in wilting away now. "She's obviously done it before. What difference does it make now?"

"You've truly told them nothing, have you Dya," Kalae croaked, in genuine surprise. "Living in both worlds is impossible. The transformation is such a strain. It rips apart bone and muscle almost instantly, then rebuilds them just as quickly. It is a brutal process. Dya has already punished her body past the point anyone should have been able to survive. If you were to see the monstrous, malformed abomination she would become if she were to attempt such an existence you would cave in the wretch's head out of mercy."

Mary Louise turned toward Dya, her face a sickly pale.

"Is this true, Dya?"

"That is why I've chosen to *stay!*" Dya screamed, and the glass in the windows finally gave way.

It was in that moment that Mary Louise noticed, for the first time, a deeper, subtler change in Dya's appearance. That in the year she had lived on land without returning to the ocean at all, she did indeed appear to have aged, if only ever so slightly, more than her four friends had. Two years for the one would seem just about right. As if she had entered more fully into young adulthood where they were still working to slough off the awkward skin of adolescence.

That will add up over time…it will certainly take its toll…

"Excuse me, sir," Ethan chimed in, "far be it from me to speak out of turn, eh. But, for whatever it's worth, I give you my word, on behalf of my friends, that we will never breathe a syllable of any of this. This is a solemn promise. Your secret and your world are safe with us. Promise."

Sarah, Malik and Molly quickly echoed the sentiment. Mary Louise simply nodded silently.

"Please let them return to Portland, Kalae," Dya said, wiping her tears on the sleeve of her T-shirt. "*Please.*"

An inscrutable expression crossed Kalae's milk-white face. His hard, cold eyes narrowed, possibly softened, though it was difficult to tell.

"And you, niece, truly do wish to return to this Port Land as well?"

Dya blinked, quite taken aback.

"Do I...Kalae? Are you asking...are you...*Yes!* Yes I want to return to Portland with them! Are you...actually...*giving your blessing*? Are you letting me go?"

"You are young, Dya," he replied, his rasping gurgle now nearly a whisper. "Young and foolish and misguided. But you are a grown woman. Too early, but you are a grown woman now. Your mistakes, tragic though they may be, are yours to make. I honor that. Come what may."

With that, Dya burst into fresh tears and ran to Mary Louise, throwing her arms around her tightly.

"I choose to stay!" Dya cried happily. "Forever!"

Mary Louise returned the hug and Dya's four other friends ran to her (Malik with help), wrapping their arms around her as a group...

However, should one have been inclined to notice, a cryptic ambiguity now simmered in Mary Louise's strained, bloodshot eyes that had not been present before.

And, indeed, Kalae did notice it. As the kids all cried tears of joy and smothered each other (and Mary Louise) in an epic embrace, the two elders silently engaged one another eye to eye from across the kitchen. Without a word spoken, each of them knew that a difficult understanding had been established between them at last.

Finally, they all stepped back away from Dya, and she approached her uncle with tremendous relief and gratitude.

"Kalae...I officially renounce my citizenship in the deep. My ability to return will fade in time, and I will fully be a woman of the land. I understand what I am giving up, and choose of my own free will this much shorter, though richer, life above the surface. Tell everyone back home that I love them, and I will miss them, and as my pulse weakens and fades from their hearts, they should be free to forget me, though I will never forget them. This is what I truly want."

Kalae nodded magnanimously.

"So be it."

And in a flash he lunged at Dya, scooped her up, threw her over his shoulder, and carried her at great speed out through the kitchen door, down the steps and off toward the ocean—as she thrashed and screamed all the way—accompanied by the other ocean men loping along close behind.

Police departments for several miles in all directions were called concerning the echoing screams that tore like sabers through the cool evening air. But ultimately no reports could be made; so brutally inhuman were the polytonal wails of rage and anguish that they could not be accurately described.

Kalae plunged into the water with Dya over his shoulder, with her still furiously attempting to free herself from his grasp. They quickly made their descent fathom by fathom, the pressure of the water around them building ever more by the minute.

All around Dya, in the pitch black of the ocean, her uncles transformed quickly back into their proper selves, their long silver tails mere flashes, whipping through the darkness.

But Dya refused to change. She would not give in to her body's aching desire to adapt to the frigid waters.

—*Do not fight the change*—Kalae chattered at her, gripping her ever harder.—*Or you will drown*—

—*You have killed me then*—she clicked and squeaked in reply.

—*I am tasked to do what is best for you*—

—*Then you have failed, you bastard*—

She would not relent, desperately struggling to maintain her feet and legs...though she feared her burning lungs would soon either burst or collapse. With a balled fist and what bit of strength she still possessed, she pounded viciously at the bridge of her uncle's nose. A red cloud shot from his nostrils, leaving a steady trail of blood as they furthered their descent.

—*I hope the sharks sniff you out and devour us both*—she snarled. But Kalae simply shook off the injury, and the blood flow ceased.

—*You are going to die—Change now*—

—*I prefer death*—

But, try though she did, she simply could not hold out any longer. With a meager exhale of resignation, she surrendered to the ocean, and was instantly overcome with a shuddering ecstasy as her legs became her tail, her lungs strengthened to withstand the pressure, and the last of her clothing ripped from her body. The glorious cold and infinite black of the deep surrounded her.

Molly, Malik, Ethan, and Sarah, devastated and numb with shock for what they had just witnessed, stood in a line along the pebble beach, gaping blankly at the now-serene calm of the evening ocean. Low tide rolled in on gentle waves breaking against the stones, and then receding again in hypnotic, clockwork repetition. Not one of them spoke, each trying to process internally what had just happened. Each wondering if they would ever see their friend again. Each suspecting that they would not.

Up the beach and away from the kids, Mary Louise watched the same tranquil tableau. A lone amethyst stone lay shimmering in the moonlight amongst the gray pebbles.

"For the best," she whispered to herself, a coating of tears resting unspilled on the lower lids of her eyes. "Goodbye, love."

How Long

Completely myself again. Truly a woman of the sea. Delirious from the opiate pleasure of my natural world...deeply ashamed for allowing myself to succumb to the pressure. I fall into blank acceptance...swim into the deep to rejoin family and pod. Here I am again back in the deep, utterly against my will. Dragged by force. Robbed of my freedom and my choice. Torn away from my friends. Threatened with their destruction, should I ever try such a thing again. So hello to the eternal sameness once again. Hello delicious narcotic chill. Hello darkness my old friend.

How long shall I stay...
  How long shall I stay...
  How long will I stay...

A Song in the Squall

After an eternity in the emergency room and a few stitches in Malik's face, it was a long, quiet drive back to Portland. Several solid hours of silent contemplation passed, with only the rain and the radio having much to say.

Finally Mary Louise said, to no one in particular,

"The road suits me. You know what I mean? It will be good to get out there again."

"Might this mean," Malik said, his jaw sore and bandaged, "that Dya's grandmother is going back home to Ukraine as well?"

"That's a good story, love," Mary Louise said. "Say that if anyone should ask. How did we settle on Ukraine anyway?"

"It was your idea. It sounds far away."

"Oh. Of course. There goes my memory again." Pause. "Should have gone with Tuscany instead. That sounds romantic."

"Will we see you again, eh?" Sarah asked.

"Let's give it a couple of years, just to be safe," Mary Louise replied. "We'll see how it all shakes out. I've got a number of falsified documents I'm going to have to bury somewhere."

"A lot?" Molly asked, speaking for the first time. Her voice thin and scratchy. "Are they traceable?"

"Well," Mary Louise replied, "I *am* currently in possession of a birth certificate for someone born in 1988. That wouldn't be so odd if I didn't clearly remember dancing with her in 1951.

Funny that."

"Nothing short of fire's gonna clear up that little clerical error," Malik said.

"That is the plan. In all likelihood a few questions will be asked, an inquiry or two, and we will be forgotten. Like nothing happened."

"Cuz nothing did, eh," Ethan said.

"Because nothing did."

Back at school, no one knew why the remaining seventy-five percent of Leviathan Immortal indifferently dismissed questions of when they might be playing out again. Or, later, if they were in the market for a new lead vocalist. They were not.

No one knew where that strange new girl had gone, and anyone likely to ask one of her four friends who sat quietly at lunch together (but seldom actually spoke) where she might be were met with a collective shrug off and some cryptic muttering about how she had in fact gone home to Kiev.

"So she really was foreign, eh?"

"Duh."

No one knew what the four of them were plotting when they would whisper to one another in the alcove by the old labs. And indeed if these four had ever looked inclined to 'go Columbine,' it would most certainly have been now. Yet, ironically enough, that insult was never lobbed at any of them again. No one knew for sure why, but no one was interested in being the one to question it.

And no one knew why the hottest boy at school, the A+ of the

A Crowd, came to the Spring Dance alone, and sat alone, and ate alone, and did not speak, and did not dance once all night. No one asked. He didn't tell.

No one could possibly ever know, nor indeed know enough to even ask, about what had happened over Spring Break near Bar Harbor. And no one ever did.

A return to their normal lives—such as they were—was genuinely attempted. The four tried to not bring Dya up in conversation, for so much of all their prior talk had concerned their grand schemes for the future. A future that involved all five pieces. Now, what else could really be said? So bonded now did the four of them feel to one another by this shared experience, whatever it was, whatever it meant, that they likely could not have made new friends even if they had wanted to.

The loss felt less like a friend had moved away, and much more like a friend had died. They were sure she was gone forever. And although they had grown closer together, their shared loss, and their sworn silence, hung like a heavy burden on all of their necks.

"We make a promise here and now, eh," Ethan said one day in the alcove by the old labs, "that the four of us will always stay together. Always. Come what may."

All agreed.

But, of course, they all knew just how delicate and breakable promises could be.

Weeks passed in much the same fashion, indistinguishable from one to the next. The end of the school year loomed in the distance, and whatever uncertainty would come along it. Then, one morning, Malik's phone chimed just prior to the crack of dawn.

"Hmmmm...'ullo?!"

"Mal?"

It was Molly.

"What up, homie?" Malik replied, his eyes still shut, the phone resting on his face free-of-hand. Though it no longer hurt, his still-bandaged jaw was stiff and a bit difficult to move. Especially at this time of the day.

"We need to go see her. Before she *disappears for good*."

"Huh? See who?"

"Mary Louise, of course."

"Oh. Uh...It's real early, babe..."

"And she's leaving. Today. I just have this feeling that she's leaving today. And if we don't talk to her before she goes, we might not ever get the chance again."

"Um, yeah but...I mean, her good-bye felt pretty final, you know? I think that maybe we should just—"

"*No!* We can't just let her disappear without..."

"Without what, Moll?"

"I...still have questions for her, Malik. I just need to talk with her, eh."

"Well...okay, but..."

"Please, Mal. *Please*. We have to go now. Right now."

"All right. All right. I'll be right over."

Molly's instincts, as they often tended to be, were correct. After laying on the buzzer for several straight minutes, one of Mary Louise's neighbors finally came out to let her and Malik in.

They rushed up the stairs to discover, not only was Mary Louise gone, but the apartment was empty. Barren. As if no one had ever lived there.

"We're too late," Malik said.

"Almost," Molly answered.

They drove around Portland proper for hours on end with nothing but a hunch to go on, missing school entirely (not that it much mattered). All for just one more 'so long,' or 'fair thee well.' Or something. For just a bit of closure. For there had been none.

Finally, after nearly accepting defeat, they spotted the Honda Civic. No mistaking it, packed as it was with Mary Louise's belongings. Not everything, of course. Just the needed things. And nothing else. Nothing decorative or superfluous.

East End Beach at the Eastern Promenade is where they found her, sitting serenely on a beaten old wooden bench, staring off into Casco Bay.

As they slowly walked up behind her, they could just barely make out the song she sang to herself.

"*...And ours is a road that is strewn with goodbyes / but as it unfolds / as it all unwinds...*"

"Mary Louise?"

"It looks so calm," she said, not turning around. "Doesn't it?"

Indeed it did. Looking out across the bay, Molly and Malik saw the sailboats and tourist ferries floating atop the surface of the water like plastic toys across a sheet of glass. The midday sun an ever-reddening orange.

But, off in the distance, dark shelf clouds rolled slowly. Lurking. Faint, but insistent.

"Storm's coming, eh," Molly said as she and Malik sat down on the bench on each side of her.

"Oh, it has already started, love. Underwater."

They sat, watching the barely moving tableau for a while. Finally Mary Louise said, "She's calm too. She is calm down there. She's not happy...I know she isn't. But she is more despondent than distressed. Or afraid. If she is being punished, it must not be too severe."

Yet...

"How do you know?" Malik asked.

"*Because,*" Mary Louise replied, her hand on her heart, her voice barely a whisper, "*I can feel her.*"

"Have...have you always?"

"Since as long as I can remember."

"Memories aren't always honest," Malik said.

"And that's not such a bad thing, hon. And neither, sometimes, are secrets. You both realize that, yes?"

She gave them each a respective sideways glance. They both looked straight ahead, not engaging the look. She grinned wryly to herself.

"What more can you tell us?" Molly asked. "In the time that you've known her, surely she's given you some idea of what it's like down there, eh? What comes now? For her? For them? For *anyone?*"

"A great storm is indeed brewing," Mary Louise said. "Of that I have no doubt. And it's churning deep in the ocean. Miles beneath the surface. So deep, none of us could survive. We'd be crushed. And frozen."

"Why? I mean, why is there trouble stirring now of all times? What's so different now, eh?"

"You must understand, hon. You have to understand the depths of her trespass. By the standards of her people, she is beyond obstinate. Disobedient. Disrespectful, not just to her elders and her minders, but of the ancient ways. And they don't know what to do about her. They won't be able to agree about how to handle this. They're afraid it may be catching. Their fears may prove justified."

"There are schisms in the deep," Malik asked, though it was not really a question.

"All cultures have schisms," Mary Louise replied. "Ideas clash. *Ideals* clash. Values collide. Action meets with reaction.

And then counter-reaction. Fierce. Violent. Deadly even, on occasion, though I pray not now. It's as inevitable as the tides. And in this case, it is sure to cause the tides to rise." Her gaze fixed again on the lightly rippling waters. She continued, "Her gifts were rare. Only a few in her culture have that power. The voice. The songs. It is a trait specific to just a few remaining families."

"How come, eh?"

"It's no longer an active part of their culture. Its purpose is ultimately cruel and savage…destructive…beautiful though it may be."

"But still an honored tradition," Malik said. "And what folks won't do for tradition…"

Mary Louise nodded.

"She was special for her talent. Practically a living antique. A living incarnation of ancient glory. And for her to just discard that, to shrug off what is so sacred to them…it is an insult beyond comprehension."

"Might we be blamed, eh?" Molly asked, trying and failing to mask a gulp in her throat. "Could there be anger aimed at…us? Like, directly?"

"I don't know," Mary Louise. But the tone in her voice said, *Most definitely. Let there be no doubt about it.*

"So then what do we do?"

"I am attempting to erase her footprints in the sand," Mary Louise replied. "And whatever you can do to help with that I would much appreciate. Thankfully, there aren't many footprints to erase." Pause. "Not like before…" she added, cryptically. "Time will tell, I suppose."

Mary Louise moved to stand. Molly and Malik did likewise.

"You're leaving?" Molly asked, her eyes red and watery, even more blurry than usual. Mary Louise hugged her.

"Much to do, hon," she said.

"Where will you go?"

"Somewhere with a shore," she said. "Always. Because you

never know, right?"

She turned to Malik and hugged him as well. Looking in his eyes, she smiled, gently touching the thin white bandage that ran along the right side of his jaw. "You know, you do have your grandfather's chin."

"I know."

"Has anyone ever told you that you look just a little tiny bit like Elmore James?"

"I'm not sure I know who that is," he replied.

"We'll get you up to speed, babe," Molly said with a grin and a squeeze of his hand.

"Careful for the storm, kids," Mary Louise said as she walked toward her car.

"You too," they answered in unison.

"Ah, Portland," Mary Louise sighed as she opened her driver's side door. "I will miss you. Alas. But, who knows. *Resurgam.*"

"*Resurgam,*" Molly whispered to herself.

"Windstorms can rise up in a moment, you know," Mary Louise said. "Often without warning. And even when it seems to have died down, it can rise up again. Listen when they come. Listen close to the music of the wind. You might just hear a voice singing as it rolls off the sea. But keep your feet planted firmly on the ground. Listen for the song in the squall...It is up to you to not get swept away."

And off she went. This time for good. Her tail lights fading into the thickening fog.

As the skies darkened further and the wind took on an ever sharper bite, Molly and Malik walked hand in hand down East End Beach, Malik with a slight but noticeable limp. They walked on, ignoring the signs of worsening weather all around. Their hair whipped wildly about their heads, unruly and swirling, much like their thoughts.

"*Blowing our wandering hearts like a feather...*" Molly sang quietly to herself.

She had the urge to peel off her checkered Chuck Taylors and wade into the waters as they grew rough and choppy. She resisted the temptation, and instead held tight to Malik's hand, almost as if she were afraid that if she were to let go of him he might just fly off and away from her.

They didn't speak. They didn't have to. Any fears, or questions, or secrets or confessions that may have lingered between them could wait for another day. Instead they just listened to the wind. Listened closely, as it grew louder and louder. They listened for music, for a song, rolling in on the wind from out deep in the sea. They didn't hear it. It wasn't there. Yet.

Just give it time. Just give it time.

Acknowledgments

Big thanks to: Eric Campbell, Lance Wright, and all the fine folks at Down & Out Books. To Elizabeth Jenike, Philip Rogers, Eric Beebe, Stephanie Kania-Beebe and the whole Post Mortem cadre. To Carolyn Haines, Greg Petersen, Yishai Seidman, Gary Heidt, Stephen Leigh, and Jessica McHugh. To Andrea Scarpino and all my Union classmates. To The Whiskey Shambles, Carian, Performance Gallery, and the ever-more awesome Cincinnati art/theatre/music/lit scene—don't stop a-rockin'! To David Gray, High on Fire, Ray LaMontagne, Mastodon, and the Elmore James estate—thanks (in advance) for not suing, and for all the great music. And, of course, all of my friends and family for continuing to put up with this, *especially* Julie, Levi and Wolf. Enjoy!

NATHAN SINGER is a novelist, playwright, composer, and experimental performing artist. He is also the lead vocalist and guitarist for award-winning "ultra-blues" band The Whiskey Shambles. His published novels are the controversial and critically-acclaimed *A Prayer for Dawn, Chasing the Wolf, In the Light of You, Blackchurch Furnace, The Song in the Squall,* and *Transorbital.* He currently lives in Cincinnati, Ohio where he is working on a multitude of new projects.

On the following pages are a few
more great titles from the
Down & Out Books publishing family.

For a complete list of books and to
sign up for our newsletter,
go to DownAndOutBooks.com.

The Better of the Bad
A Trevor Galloway Thriller
J.J. Bensley

Down & Out Books
October 2020
978-1-64396-149-1

He dials 9-1-1, calls the dispatch center at exactly 9:11 PM, and provides the location. By then, it's too late for anyone to help. Another dispatcher will have lost someone close to them. The murders happen quickly, brutally, and on schedule.

Trevor Galloway and Bethany Nolan have been hired to stop the terror that is plaguing the Savannah area, but at what cost?

Third Degree
Ross Klavan, Tim O'Mara and Charles Salzberg

Down & Out Books
October 2020
978-1-64396-162-0

Cut Loose All Those Who Drag You Down by Ross Klavan. A crooked reporter who fronts for the mob is in deep trouble and it's clear somebody is going to pay with his life.

Beaned by Tim O'Mara. Aggie discovers a sinister plot to exploit what some consider a precious commodity: the trafficking of under-aged children for the purposes of sex.

The Fifth Column by Charles Salzberg. A young reporter uncovers that the recently disbanded German-American Bund might still be active and is planning a number of dangerous actions on American soil.

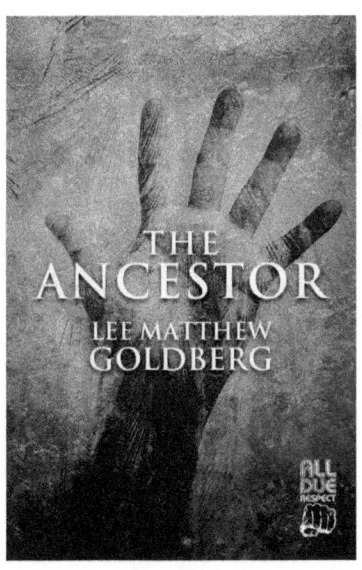

The Ancestor
Lee Matthew Goldberg

All Due Respect, an imprint of
Down & Out Books
August 2020
978-1-64396-114-9

A man wakes up in the Alaskan wilderness with no memory of who he is, except for the belief that he's was a prospector from the Gold Rush and has been frozen in ice for over a hundred years.

A meditation on love lost and unfulfilled dreams, *The Ancestor* is a thrilling page-turner in present day Alaska and a historical adventure about the perilous Gold Rush expeditions where prospectors left behind their lives for the promise of hope and a better future.

Deemer's Inlet
Stephen Burdick

Shotgun Honey, an imprint of
Down & Out Books
August 2020
978-1-64396-104-0

Far from the tourist meccas of Ft. Lauderdale and Miami Beach, a chief of police position in the quiet, picturesque town of Deemer's Inlet on the Gulf coast of Florida seemed ideal for Eldon Quick—until the first murder.

The crime and a subsequent killing force Quick to call upon his years of experience as a former homicide detective in Miami. Soon after, two more people are murdered and Quick believes a serial killer is on the loose. As Quick works to uncover the identity and motive of the killer, he must contend with an understaffed police force, small town politics, and curious residents.

www.ingramcontent.com/pod-product-compliance
Lightning Source LLC
Chambersburg PA
CBHW020254030426
42336CB00010B/759